After his first year of retirement Tom Weber wrote *Retiremental!* with the hope of helping family and friends with their own retirements. Tom is currently retired and living in Deerwood, Minnesota, with his wife Sue. Together they have two adult children: Ben, Abby, and her husband, Zander. They are also the proud grandparents of their grandson, Hunter!

To Sue

For your patience and inspiration throughout this project and your love throughout my life.

Tom Weber

RETIREMENTAL!

Quotes and Quips of Wit and Wisdom
for the Newly and Oldly Retired

AUSTIN MACAULEY PUBLISHERS™
LONDON • CAMBRIDGE • NEW YORK • SHARJAH

Copyright © Tom Weber 2024

All rights reserved. No part of this publication may be reproduced, distributed, or transmitted in any form or by any means, including photocopying, recording, or other electronic or mechanical methods, without the prior written permission of the publisher, except in the case of brief quotations embodied in critical reviews and certain other non-commercial uses permitted by copyright law. For permission requests, write to the publisher.

Any person who commits any unauthorized act in relation to this publication may be liable to criminal prosecution and civil claims for damages.

Ordering Information
Quantity sales: Special discounts are available on quantity purchases by corporations, associations, and others. For details, contact the publisher at the address below.

Publisher's Cataloging-in-Publication data
Weber, Tom
Retiremental!

ISBN 9798886932591 (Paperback)
ISBN 9798886932607 (ePub e-book)

Library of Congress Control Number: 2023918295

www.austinmacauley.com/us

First Published 2024
Austin Macauley Publishers LLC
40 Wall Street, 33rd Floor, Suite 3302
New York, NY 10005
USA

mail-usa@austinmacauley.com
+1 (646) 5125767

Welcome to Retiremental!

Retiremental! is a light-hearted and heartfelt book that blends adages and axioms, quotes and quips, aphorisms and witticisms. Some informative. Some entertaining. Some serious. Some tongue-in-cheek. Some inspirational. Some thought-provoking. All designed to assist you throughout the retirement realm.

Most books on the subject of retirement deal predominately with financial and healthcare information. Although these subjects are of the utmost importance, ***Retiremental!*** covers retirement in a more holistic way.

Retiremental! Will provide you with advice to reduce the challenges of retirement as you encounter new roles, new relationships and new routines.

Someday we will all retire, and we all desire and deserve a happy and fulfilling retirement. It is my sincere hope that ***Retiremental!*** will enable you to not just survive, but thrive in the second half of your life.

Happy Retirement!
Tom Weber

Adventure

"Today is your day! Your mountain is awaiting! So… get on your way."
– Dr. Seuss

"Climb the mountain so that you can see the world, not so the world can see you."
– Anonymous

"Adventure is worthwhile in itself."
– Amelia Earhart

"The biggest adventure you can take is to live the life of your dreams."
– Oprah Winfrey

"When was the last time you did something for the first time?"
– Darius Rucker

"Never stop doing things for the first time."
– Anonymous

"Life is either a daring adventure or nothing."
– Helen Keller

"Adventures start where plans end!"
– Anonymous

"It's never too late in life to have a genuine adventure."
– Robert Kurson

"If you think adventure is dangerous, try routine, it's lethal."
– Paulo Coelho

"Put one dumb foot in front of the other and course correct as you go."
– Barry Diller

"I get up in the morning looking for an adventure."
– George Foreman

"Retirement—the final frontier. These are the adventures of the newly and oldly retired. Their lifetime mission is to explore strange new worlds, seek out a new life, and to boldly go where no retiree has gone before."
– Tom Weber

"Blessed are the curious for they shall have adventures."
– Lovelle Drachman

"The only way of discovering the limits of the possible is to venture a little way past them into the impossible."
– Arthur C. Clark

"Life is an adventure, it's not a package tour."
– Eckhart Tolle

Aging

"Some people age like wine, others like milk."

— Tumblr

"Aging is an extraordinary process where you become the person you always should have been."

— David Bowie

"Your age is like a price tag. The higher it gets the more valuable you are."

— Anonymous

"Anyone who keeps the ability to see beauty never grows old."

— Franz Kafka

"Age is an issue of mind over matter. If you don't mind, it doesn't matter."

— Mark Twain

"Live your life and forget your age."

— Norman Vincent Peale

"Age is nothing but experience, and some are more experienced than others."

— Andy Rooney

"Inside every retiree is a teenager asking: 'What the hell happened?'"

— Anonymous

"My inner child just turned sixty-five."

— Sidney Harris

"Aging seems to be the only available way to live a long life."

– Daniel-Francois-Esprit Auber

"For the unlearned, old age is winter; for the learned, it is the season of the harvest."

– Hasidic Saying

"First you forget names, then you forget faces; then you forget to sip your fly, then you forget to unzip your fly."

– Branch Rickey

"There are three signs of old age. Loss of memory… I forget the other two."

– Red Skelton

"Of all the self-fulfilling prophecies in our culture, the assumption that aging means decline and poor health is probably the deadliest."

– Marilyn Ferguson

"Just live your life and don't be influenced by society trying to make you feel some way about your age."

– Madonna

"It's not how old you are, but how you are old."

– Marie Dressler

"The only 100% effective way to reverse aging is to falsify your birth certificate."
– Tom Weber

Contradiction Alert!
"Age is just a number. False: Age is a word."
– Dwight Schrute: from "The Office"

Aging Acceptance

"It's better to be 65 years young than 40 years old."
– Jimmy Carter

"The age of a woman doesn't mean a thing. The best tunes are played on the oldest fiddles."
– Sigmund Z. Engel

"You're not getting old. You are old."
– Tom Weber

"Age happens. No matter how much money you spend in damage control, how healthy you eat, or what vitamins you take, age happens."
– Annie Keys

"Stop whining about getting old. It's a privilege."
– Amy Poehler

**"Be comfortable in your own skin,
even if your birthday suit needs some ironing."**
– Tom Weber

Contradiction Alert!
"Now you understand why Peter Pan didn't want to grow up."
– Anonymous

"I refuse to admit that I am more than 52,
even if that does make my sons illegitimate."
– Mary Astor

Aging Gracefully

"The trick to aging gracefully is to enjoy it."

– Anonymous

"If someone forgets your birthday, take it as a compliment. You must not have aged enough to be noticed."

– Anonymous

"I've learned that the secret of growing old gracefully is never to lose your enthusiasm for meeting new people and seeing new places."

– Anonymous

"Oh Vanity. Let me age gracefully and with acceptance."

– Tom Weber

"I don't know how to act my age. I've never been this age before."
– Tumblr

Contradiction Alert!
"I don't plan to grow old gracefully.
I plan to have facelifts until my ears meet."
– Rita Rudner

Age-ism

"Age-ism is as odious as racism and sexism."

– Claude Peppers

Smash Age-ist stereotypes. Be a new role model for others. Be more physically active, socially active, and mentally active than the stereotypes suggest.

"Hiding or lying about your age is giving in to ageism. Don't do it! Be proud of who you are, what you know and what you've accomplished."

– John Tarnoff

Never accept second-class status.

"I have no need to conform to the stereotypes others have defined for me."

– Jonathan Lockwood Huie

"R.I.P. traditional views of retirement and archaic myths of old age."

– Tom Weber

"Ageism is getting old."

– Bumper Sticker

Do not accept Age-ism, but understand the ignorance behind the behavior.

"The one way to avoid age discrimination in Hollywood is to die young."

– Larry Gelbart

"Discrimination on the basis of age is as unacceptable as discrimination on the basis of any other aspect of ourselves that we cannot change."

– Ashton Applewhite

Help stop Age-ism. Take the time to tactfully educate and explain why something is Age-ist.

> **"Please don't call me 'Honey' or 'Sweetie',**
> **and I won't call you 'Condescending' or 'Patronizing'."**
> – Tom Weber

Attitude

"Too blessed to be stressed."

– John Mulaney

"Life isn't about your age. Life is about living. So, when your birthday comes, be thankful for the year that has just past, and anticipate with a happy heart what the coming year will bring."

– Catherine Pulsifer

"Today's Forecast: 100% chance of winning!"

– Anonymous

"We all have our crosses we must bear, but just don't let them crucify you."

– Tom Weber

"There's a whole new kind of life ahead, full of experiences just waiting to happen. Some call it 'Retirement'. I call it bliss."

– Betty Sullivan

"Let that shit go."

– Bumper Sticker

"We can always choose to perceive things differently. You can focus on what's wrong in your life, or you can focus on what's right."

– Marianne Williamson

"The Dude abides."

– The Stranger: from *The Big Lebowski*

"Every little thing gonna be alright!"

– Bob Marley

"Nevertheless, she persisted."
– Mitch McConnell

"Attitude is the difference between ordeal and adventure."
– Bob Bitchin

"Know that you are the perfect age. Each year is special and precious, for you shall only live it once."
– Louise Hay

"'I like it when retirees grumble and complain'—said no one ever."
– Tom Weber

"Don't sweat the petty things and don't pet the sweaty things."
– George Carlin

"A lion chased me up a tree, and I greatly enjoyed the view from the top."
– Confucius

"The longer I live, the more beautiful life becomes."
– Frank Lloyd Wright

"If life seems jolly rotten.
There's something you've forgotten.
And that's to laugh and smile and dance and sing
When you're feeling in the dumps, don't be silly chumps.
Just purse your lips and whistle—that's the thing
And… Always look on the bright side of life."
– Monty Python

"When you count your blessings, count retirement twice."
– Tom Weber

Authenticity

"You can't fake authenticity."

– Button

"Authenticity is a collection of choices that we must make every day. It's about the choice to show up and be real. The choice to be honest. The choice to let our true selves be seen."

– Brene Brown

"Be yourself, everyone else is taken."

– Oscar Wilde

"We should be authentic: the 'real deal'. Neither a clone nor mimic be."

– Fennel Hudson

"And so, become yourself, because the past is just a good bye."

– Crosby, Stills, Nash, and Young

"Don't trade in your authenticity for approval."

– Anonymous

"Whether I'm right or whether I'm wrong
Whether I find a place in this world or never belong
I gotta be me, I've gotta be me
What else can I be but what I am."

– Walter Marks

"To be nobody but myself—in a world which is doing its best, night and day, to make me somebody else—means to fight the hardest battle any human can fight, and never stop fighting."

– e. e. cummings

"It's okay if you don't like me. Not everyone has good taste."

– Anonymous

"The older I get, the more I understand that it's okay to live life others don't understand."

– Iain Morland

"Don't worry about what's cool and what's not cool. Authenticity is what's cool."
– Zac Posen

Contradiction Alert!
"Accept who you are. Unless you're a serial killer!"
– Ellen Degeneres

"Those are my principles, if you don't like them, I have others."
– Groucho Marx

The Blues

Retirement is not always peachy keen. Accept the fact that occasionally you will have a bad day. But don't wait too long to start smiling again. Start by taking a small positive step, moving forward from whatever it is that is troubling you. This meaningful action may not solve your problem completely, but you'll be on your way to happiness and better days.

"Sadness: nothing a bit of shopping can't fix."
– Bumper Sticker

"Sadness is a necessary emotion. It maybe not the most pleasant one to have, but it's cathartic."
– Phyllis Smith

"The word 'happy 'would lose its meaning if it were not balanced by sadness."
– Carl Jung

"Faking a smile is so much easier than explaining why you are sad."
– Anonymous

"Dear Sadness, I think you should take a vacation. Believe me, you are not gonna be missed."
– Tom Weber

"I want to feel what I feel. Even if it's not happiness."
– Toni Morrison

"You know you're getting old when all the names in your black book have M.D. after them."
– Arnold Palmer

"Put cotton in your ears and pebbles in your shoes. Pull on rubber gloves. Smear Vaseline over your glasses, and there you have it: instant old age."

– Malcolm Cowley

"When you're happy you enjoy the music. When you're sad you understand the lyrics."

– Anonymous

"Before you diagnose yourself with depression or low self-esteem, first make sure that you are not in fact, just surrounding yourself with assholes."
– Anonymous

Boredom

"Bored of being bored because being bored is boring."
– Bumper Sticker

"Boredom is a disease."
– Tommy Chong

"I've got a great ambition, to die of exhaustion rather than boredom."
– Thomas Carlyle

"Without new experiences, something inside of us sleeps."
– Anonymous

"Discussing how old you are is the temple of boredom."
– Ruth Gordon

"The cure for boredom is curiosity. There is no cure for curiosity."
– Dorthy Parker

"You don't want your obituary to read: 'Died of Boredom'."
– Tom Weber

Bucket List

"Always have something on your Bucket List."

– Mall walker

Along with your individual Bucket Lists, make a separate Bucket List with your spouse or partner.

"Create a Bucket List before you kick it!"

– Tom Weber

"My only goal in retirement is to cross off things from my bucket list and update it again."

– Refrigerator Magnet

"Put yourself at the top of your to-do list every single day and the rest will fall into place."

– Anonymous

"The Bucket List. All other lists pail in comparison."

– Tom Weber

"Have a 'Fucket List!' A 'To Don't Do List' of tasks, activities, or obligations that you plan to quit doing in retirement."
– Tom Weber

Contradiction Alert!
"I don't keep a Bucket List. I'm open to anything."
– Anonymous

Busyness

"I'm so busy since I have retired, I may have to go back to work to get a rest."
— Uncle Dude

"Trade your busy life for a full one."
— Anonymous

"Replace F.O.M.O. (Fear of Missing Out) with J.O.M.O. (Joy of Missing Out)!"
— Anonymous

"All work and no play makes Jack a dull boy."
— Jack Torrance: from *The Shining*

"May I never get too busy in my own affairs that I fail to respond to the needs of others with kindness and compassion."
— Thomas Jefferson

"The quality of the activity is more important than the quantity of activities."
— Tom Weber

"When we get too caught up in the busyness of the world, we lose connection with one another—and ourselves."
— Jack Kornfield

"Stop the glorification of busy!"
— Bumper Sticker

"Life is what happens while you are busy making other plans."
— John Lennon

"I really stay busy in retirement. I often have to cancel my golf games on the weekends to go play in a tennis tournament."

– Richard Davies

"I wanted to figure out why I was so busy, but I couldn't find the time to do it."
– Todd Stocker

Contradiction Alert!
Stay busy. You will be less likely to be bored if you engage in meaningful activities.

Coffee

"I don't need an inspirational quote, what I need is a freaking cup of coffee."
— Anonymous

"Inertia happens, but coffee helps."
— Tom Weber

"Genius doesn't happen on decaf."
— Words on Coffee Mug

"Coffee is a beverage that puts one to sleep when not drank."
— Alphonse Allais

"I don't need to drink coffee to be awesome. I'm already awesome. But it's more fun when I'm awesome and awake."
— Anonymous

"Coffee helps me maintain my never killed anyone streak."
— Words on Coffee Mug

"Coffee! Because anger management is too expensive."
— Anonymous

"When I wake up in the morning, I just can't get started until I've had that first, piping hot pot of coffee. Oh, I've tried other enemas."

– Emo Phillips

"A yawn is a silent scream for coffee."

– Anonymous

"Coffee is so important that they named a table after it."

– Gary Gulman

"Life without coffee is like something without something… sorry, I haven't had any coffee yet."

– Anonymous

"Depresso: the feeling you get when you run out of coffee."

– Bumper Sticker

"I'm not addicted to coffee, we're just in a committed relationship."

– Words on Coffee Mug

"Almost all my middle-aged and elderly acquaintances, including me, feel about 25, unless we haven't had our coffee, in which case we feel 107."

– Martha Beck

"Procaffeinating: to delay or postpone actions: put off doing something until you've had coffee."

– Anonymous

Communication

Pontification gets old. If someone asks for the time—don't tell them how to make a watch.

"Learn when's a good time to shut up."
— Dr. Phil

"Having the maturity to know sometimes silence is more powerful than having the last word."
— Anonymous

Retirement Resolution: avoid digressions. You're only interrupting yourself.

Be patient with yourself, and others, when experiencing Tip of the Tongue Syndrome.

"In the good old days…" and "When I was your age…" stories should not hijack a conversation.

Health updates are okay, but don't let your conversation become an "Organ Recital" of ailments and aches. Create a self-imposed time limit for yourself.

"If you cannot be positive, then at least be quiet."
— Joel Osteen

"A closed mouth gathers no feet."
— Fortune Cookie

A "Globe Talker" is a retiree who loves talking about the places they've been to and where they'll be going. Although it is not the intent, it may come across as bragging.

"A good conversation is like a mini-skirt, short enough to keep your interest, but long enough to cover the subject."

– Anonymous

"Create a 'Bitch Card'. You get your 'Bitch Card' punched when you complain about something. You get one punch per day on your card."

– Mark Weber

"Your tongue is your ambassador."

– Fortune Cookie

Retirees can sometimes repeat themselves—repeat themselves. So introduce stories with "Stop me if you've heard this before." if you're not sure that you've already told it.

"Oh, I'm so sorry. Did the middle of my sentence interrupt the beginning of yours?"
– Button

Courage

"Courage is being scared to death, but saddling up anyway."
— John Wayne

"Living in fear is not living at all."
— Christopher Reeve

"Do ya think Lewis and Clark had a map?"
— Ben Weber

"Everything you've ever wanted is on the other side of fear."
— George Addair

"Life shrinks or expands in proportion to one's courage."
— Anais Nin

"Nothing in life is to be feared. It is only to be understood."
— Marie Curie

"Don't be afraid to take a big step if one is indicated. You can't cross a chasm in two small jumps."
— David Lloyd George

"Fear is for people who don't get out very much."
— Rick Steves

"Fearlessness is not the absence of fear. It's the mastery of fear."
— Arianna Huffington

"Curiosity will conquer fear even more than bravery will."
— James Stephens

"Eighty percent of all choices are based on fear. Most people don't choose what they want; they choose what they think is safe."

– Dr. Phil

"All glory comes from daring to begin."

– Helen Keller

"What we fear doing most is usually what we most need to do."

– Tim Ferriss

"There's only one terrifying fact about old people: I'm gonna be one soon."
– P. J. O'Rourke

Creativity

"It's impossible to explain creativity. It's like asking a bird 'How do you fly?' You just do."

– Eric Jerome Dickey

Express yourself artistically. Paint, sculpt, write, cook, compose…

Restore something: a piece of heirloom furniture, a classic motorcycle, vintage clothing…

It's never too late to get the creative juices flowing and release your creative spirit.

"The objective is not to become a published poet or a concert pianist. Rather, it's to gain an outlet for all the creativity that used to be applied to work."

– Sara Yogev

Do it for the experience—not the results. Mastery isn't necessary.

Gift your creative work or sell it.

"Creativity is intelligence having fun."

– Albert Einstein

"Creativity is a bottomless well."
– Phil Bolsta

Decompression from Work

"It's normal to feel some P.W.S.D. = Post Work Stress Disorder."
– Tom Weber

Detach. Let go the stress and pressures you faced at work.

Give yourself time to decompress from your job.

It's normal to have mixed feelings or feeling out of sync about what you're leaving, even if you are moving on to something good.

"Develop work amnesia."
– Tom Weber

Pretending to not miss work, when you do, is a mistake.

Find other outlets to give your life new meaning and a sense of purpose.

Try mentoring or volunteering.

"Get off the 'Stress Express'."
– Dave Albers

Doing Nothing

"Rest is not idleness, and to lie sometimes on the grass under the trees on a summer's day, listening to the murmur of water, or watching the clouds float across the blue sky, is by no means a waste of time."
– John Lubbock

"How beautiful it is to do nothing, and then rest afterward."
– Spanish Proverb

"Retirement: when you stop lying about your age and start lying around the house."
– Anonymous

"The trouble with doing nothing is you never know when you're done."
– Robin Ryan

"When you get older, it takes a lot longer to do nothing."
– Catharine Brandt

"Relax, recharge and reflect. Sometimes it's OK to do nothing."
– Izey Victoria Odiase

"There's never enough time to do all the nothing you want."
– Bill Watterson

"It's astonishing how long it takes to finish something you are not working on."

– Button

"Despite what you might believe, it is quite productive to do absolutely nothing."

– Anonymous

"Doing nothing in a hot tub has added benefits."

– Anonymous

"Retirement is wonderful. It's doing nothing without worrying about getting caught at it."

– Gene Perret

"It's never too late to do nothing at all."

– Allen Ginsberg

"I love to work at nothing all day."
– Bachman-Turner Overdrive

Encore Employment

An encore job is a second career that someone has after retiring from their first career. Encore employment isn't just about generating income, it's also about doing something meaningful, enjoyable, and rewarding. Encore co-workers are a new source for potential friends. Test the waters before you plunge head first into an encore experience, and remember encore employment is a revolving door. Feel free to go in and out.

Endgame

"One day your life will flash before your eyes. Make sure it's worth watching."
– Anonymous

"In the end, it's not the years in your life that count, it's the life in your years."
– Abe Lincoln

"When it comes time to die, let us not discover that we have never lived."
– Henry David Thoreau

"Remember you're retired—not expired."
– Anonymous

"You are ripe, not rotten, but let's not forget that pesky expiration date."
– Tom Weber

"Acknowledging that life is finite gives present life meaning."
– Anonymous

"It's better to be seen than viewed."
– Anonymous

"The beauty of things must be that they end."
– Jack Kerouac

Try the 'We Croak' app. Throughout the day, at five random times, this app will automatically send you inspirational and motivational quotes to remind you to live life to the fullest.

"Spoiler Alert! In the end we all get fitted for a halo."
– Tom Weber

"Every man dies but not every man really lives."
— William Wallace from *Braveheart*

"The good don't always die young."
— Bumper Sticker

"I shall pass through this world but once. Any good thing therefore that I can do or any kindness I can show to any fellow creature let me do it now. Let me not defer nor neglect it, for I shall not pass this way again."
— Stephen Grellet

"At the end of the game, the King and the Pawn go into the same box."
— Italian Proverb

Endgame

"Imagine your funeral. Are you happy with your eulogy? If not—now is the time to make some positive changes in your life."

– Tom Weber

"It's my life and it's now or never!
Cause I ain't gonna live forever!
I just want live while I'm alive!
It's my life!"

– Bon Jovi

"Always read something that will make you look good if you die in the middle of it."

– P.J. O'Rourke

"Do not take life too seriously. You will never get out of it alive."

– Elbert Hubbard

"Any day above ground is a good one."

– Bumper Sticker

"Confront a corpse at least once. The absolute absence of life is the most disturbing and challenging confrontation you will ever have."

– Dave Bowie

"When there is limited time left, there is little to lose by being totally honest."

– Bonnie Ware

"I love living. I love that I'm alive to love my age. There are many people who went to bed just as I did yesterday evening and didn't wake this morning. I love and feel very blessed that I did."

– Maya Angelou

"Everything that has a beginning has an ending. Make your peace with that and all will be well."

– Jack Kornfield

"The 3 immutable facts: You own stuff. You will die. Someone will get that stuff."

– Jane Bryant Quinn

"It's not that I'm afraid to die, I just don't want to be there when it happens."

– Woody Allen

"Life is terminal, so make it memorable."
– The Grim Reaper (Tom Weber)

Energy

"Too much ease can lead to disease."

– Anonymous

"For a quick burst of energy, end every shower with 30 seconds of a cool to cold water rinse."

– Naturopathic Medical Student

"Wake up with polka music every morning. It'll really get your blood pumping."

– Retiree in restaurant

"It's exhausting complaining about how tired I am."

– Anonymous

"Vigor till rigor!"
– Tom Weber

Contradiction Alert!

"I told the doctor, I was overtired, anxiety-ridden, compulsively active, constantly depressed, with recurring fits of paranoia. Turns out I'm normal."

– Jules Feiffer

Enthusiasm

"None are as old as they who have outlived their enthusiasm."
– Henry David Thoreau

"Catch on fire with enthusiasm and people will come from miles to watch you burn."
– Anonymous

"Enthusiasm is the yeast that raises the dough."
– Paul Meyer

"Curb your urge to curb your enthusiasm."
– Tom Weber

"Nothing great was ever achieved without enthusiasm."
– Ralph Waldo Emerson

"Age may wrinkle faces, but lack of enthusiasm wrinkles the soul."
– Danish Proverb

Escape-ism

"May I retreat into my imagination now, please?"
—Button

Welcome your daydreams.

"Thank God for fiction: the magical portal into another dimension."
—Tom Weber

"Let the music take you to places you dream of."
—Tumblr

"We need the possibility of escape as surely as we need hope."
—Edward Abbey

"Literature is my utopia."
—Hellen Keller

"Happiness is escaping reality from time to time."
—Bumper Sticker

"Go on an 'Armchair Adventure!' Vicariously: climb Mount Everest, explore the jungles of Africa, or trek to the North Pole—just by reading a book."

– Tom Weber

"I disappear into books. What's your superpower?"
– Anonymous

Contradiction Alert!
"Don't vicariously live through other's adventures.
This is your life. Live it."
– Anonymous

Everyday

Mini adventure. Mini-road trip. Mini-safari.

Mini-vacation. Mini-nap. Mini workout.

Learn something new every day.

Meet someone new every day.

Do something new every day.

Family

"It's not what you have in your life, but it's who you have in your life that counts."

– Anonymous

"Happiness is having a large, loving, caring, close-knit family in another city."

– George Burns

"Families are like fudge—mostly sweet, with a few nuts."

– Les Dawson

"If you're a part of my family, I will love you violently."

– Charlie Sheen

"If you met my family you'd understand."

– Bumper Sticker

Surround yourself with your favorite family photos.

"Family is a blessing. Just keep saying that when you are irritated by something a family member says."

– Marcelina Hardy

"One day you will do things for me that you hate. That is what it means to be family."

– Jonathan Safran Foer

"It always helps to have people we love beside us when we have to do difficult things in life."

– Mister Rogers

"A happy family is but an earlier heaven."
– John Bowring

Food

"Let food be thy medicine and medicine be thy food."

– Hippocrates

"Last night I had a typical cholesterol-free dinner: baked squash, skimmed milk, and gelatin. I'm sure this will not make me live any longer, but I know it's going to seem longer."

– Groucho Marx

"Do a fast-food fast."

– Tom Weber

"Money can't buy happiness, but it can buy chocolate and that's kind of the same thing."

– Bumper Sticker

"I need the yoga of food to take me away."

– Andrew Zimmern

"If we're not meant to have midnight snacks, why is there a light in the fridge?"

– Button

"Don't dig your grave with your own knife and fork."
– Anonymous

**"I stay away from natural foods.
At my age, I need all the preservatives I can get."**
– George Burns

Fountain of Youth

"Exercise is the Fountain of Youth."

– Anonymous

"Chuck Norris found the Fountain of Youth, but he wasn't thirsty."

– Tumblr

"The secret of the Fountain of Youth is to think youthful thoughts."

– Josephine Baker

"Forget about the Fountain of Youth. What we need is the Fountain of Martinis."

– Greeting Card

"The Fountain of Youth is in your mind."

– Sophia Loren

**"I have discovered the Fountain of Youth.
And it looks and tastes a lot like wine."**
– Refrigerator Magnet

Contradiction Alert!
"Who needs the Fountain of Youth.
I'm searching for the Fountain of Health."
– Tom Weber

Friends

"We need old friends to help us grow old, and new friends to help us stay young."
– Letty Cottin Pogrebin

"Our intimate friendships shield us from loneliness."
– Judith Voirst

"Friendship is like peeing on yourself: everyone can see it, but only you get the warm feeling that it brings."
– Robert Bloch

"The best vitamin for developing friends if B1."
– Anonymous

"Don't allow the grass to grow on the path of friendship."
– Native American Saying

"Count your age by friends, not years. Count your life by smiles, not tears."
– John Lennon

"Money might make you wealthy, but friends make you rich."
– Anonymous

"For those 65 and older, an active social life can increase your longevity two and a half years."

– Ted Talk

"Best friends are the siblings God chose not to give us."

– Anonymous

"A friend can't promise to fix all your problems, but they can promise that you won't have to face them all alone."

– Anonymous

**"We'll be old friends until we're old and senile.
Then we'll be new friends."**

– Tumblr

Fun

"Have some fun before the senility kicks in!"

– Bumper Sticker

"If it ain't fun don't do it."

– Jack Canfield

"Add in some fun, to get yourself to make a healthy change that you long to achieve."

– Dr. Andrew Weil

"Sometimes, having fun with your friend is all the therapy you need."

– Button

"There is no need to be bound by convention, push the envelope, do it weird, do it different, but most of all do it fun! Be that cigar chomping rock 'n' roll granny if it takes your fancy."

– Stella Rheingold

"There is no way that you were born to just pay bills and die."

– Anonymous

"Just rock on and have a good time."
— Duane Allman

"When you stop doing things for fun, you might as well be dead."
— Ernest Hemingway

"Create an adult toy chest."
— Tom Weber

"The reason adults should look as though they are having fun, is to give kids a reason to want to grow up."
— Patch Adams

"Life is meant to be fun, and joyous and fulfilling. May each of yours be that."
— Jim Henson

"We are here on Earth to fart around. Don't let anybody tell you any different."
— Kurt Vonnegut

"The best days are when you're having too much fun to take pictures."
— Anonymous

"If you don't enjoy yourself now—when will you?"
— Tom Weber

Giving

"Give with no expectation of getting something in return, and it becomes a purer, more beautiful act."

– Anonymous

Giving is so much better than getting.

Simply put: "You can't take it with you." So, you might as well give it away.

"Instead of presents, give presence."

– Leo Babauta

"Money can buy happiness—if you share it."

– Tom Weber

"We make a living by what we get; we make a life by what we give."

– Winston Churchill

"Whatever you do always give 100%—unless you're donating blood."

– Poster

"Generosity is giving more than you can, and pride is taking less than you need."

– Khalil Gibran

"Live, give, forgive."

– Rabbi Lord Jonathan Sacks

"Anything that is of value in life only multiplies when it is given."

– Deepak Chopra

"Wealth is but dung, useful only when spread around."
– Bumper Sticker

Grandparents

"Being a grandparent is your reward for not killing your kids."

– Anonymous

"What a bargain grandchildren are! I give them my loose change, and they give me a million dollars' worth of pleasure."

– Gene Perret

"Grandparents—so easy even a child can operate."

– Refrigerator Magnet

"Grandparents are like stars. You don't always see them, but you know they're there."

– Anonymous

"Grandchildren are God's way of compensating us for growing old."

– Mary H. Waldrip

"Grandparents make the world a little softer, a little kinder, and a little warmer."

– Anonymous

"Proud Parent of a Parent"

– Bumper Sticker

"Grandparents are as necessary to a child's growth as vitamins."

– Joyce Allston

"Grandparent is a little bit parent, a little bit teacher, and a little bit best friend."

– Anonymous

**"Few things are more delightful
than grandchildren fighting over your lap."**
– Doug Larson

Grandparents

"No cowboy was ever faster on the draw than a grandparent pulling a baby picture out of a wallet."

– Anonymous

"When grandparents enter the door, discipline flies out the window."

– Ogden Nash

"Elephants and grandchildren never forget."

– Andy Rooney

"My grandchild has taught me what true love means. It means watching Scooby-Doo cartoons while the basketball game is on another channel."

– Gene Perret

"A grandmother pretends she doesn't know who you are on Halloween."

– Erma Bombeck

"My grandmother is over eighty and still doesn't need glasses. Drinks right out of the bottle."

– Henny Youngman

"Grandchildren are a grandparent's link to the future. Grandparents are the child's link to the past."

– Anonymous

"All of my grandchildren are brilliant and beautiful, and obviously take after their grandmother."

– Anonymous

"I'll love you forever,
I'll like you for always.
As long as I'm living
My grand baby you'll be."

– Robert Munsch

"Grandchildren don't make a man feel old; it's the knowledge that he's married to a grandmother."

– J. Norman Collie

"The reason grandchildren and grandparents get along so well is that they have a common enemy."
– Sam Levenson

Gratitude

"Need a reason to be grateful? Check your pulse."

– Anonymous

"Expect nothing. Appreciate everything."

– Anonymous

"Life doesn't owe us anything. We only owe ourselves, to make the most of the life we are living, of the time we have left, and to live in gratitude."

– Bronnie Ware

"I am grateful for what I have. My thanksgiving is perpetual."

– Henry David Thoreau

"True gratitude is not something you feel—it's something you do."

– Anonymous

"No matter what the situation is…close your eyes and think of all the things in your life you could be grateful for right now."

– Deepak Chopra

"Start a Gratitude journal. Start each day, writing down everything you are thankful for. The struggle ends when the gratitude begins."

– Neale Donald Walsch

"Feeling gratitude and not expressing it is like wrapping a present and not giving it."

– William Arthur Ward

"If the only prayer you said in your whole life was 'Thank you', that would suffice."

– Meister Eckhart

"There's always—always—always something or someone to be thankful for."

– Tom Weber

"Gratitude always comes into play; research shows that people are happier if they are grateful for the positive things in their lives, rather than worrying about what might be missing."

– Dan Buettner

"Gratitude is the vitamin for the soul."

– Angie Karan Kresos

"Be grateful for the little things: like sleeping in freshly laundered sheets."
– Sue Weber

Guilty Pleasures

"Hang out at a busy construction site and watch people work."

– Tom Weber

"Are they still 'bad habits' if you like them?"

– Meme

"There is no pleasure worth forgoing just for an extra three years in the geriatric ward."

– John Mortimer

"Donuts. Eat more hole foods."

– Button

"When going to the bathroom, take a newspaper."

– Anonymous

"One word: BACON!"

– Tom Weber

**"What's my guilty pleasure?
The thing is, I never feel guilty about pleasures."**
– Tom Hiddleston

Hangout

Hangout at your favorite craft brewery and nurse a beer.

Hangout at your favorite spot in the library and peruse the newspapers and magazines.

Hangout at your favorite park bench and watch for shapes in the clouds.

Join the cloud Appreciation Society.

Hang out reminiscing with old friends.

Hangout on your favorite outdoor patio and nurse an iced tea.

Hangout at your favorite coffee shop and nurse a coffee.

Hangout at your favorite winery and nurse a glass of wine.

> **"My wife doesn't mind if I hang around at home. However, she gets mad if I try to come inside."**
> – A retiree who wishes to remain anonymous

Happily Ever After

"And they lived happily (aside from a few normal disagreements, misunderstandings, pouts, silent treatments, and unexpected calamities) ever after."

— Jean Ferris

"Maybe it's a fairy tale, but I believe in happily ever after."

— Jennifer Aniston

"Happily, ever after doesn't come easy. But for love, it's always worth the fight."

— M. Leighton

"After going through years of litigation to get royalties due to him, the guy who coined the term 'happily ever after' lived reasonably well for a while."

— Demetri Martin

"Don't bother me. I'm living happily ever after."

— Bumper Sticker

"Happily, ever after is not a fairy tale. It's a choice."

— Fawn Weaver

"Each happy ending's a brand-new beginning."

— Enchanted

"It's never too late to live happily ever after."

— Anonymous

"It is only possible to live happily ever after on a daily basis."

— Margaret Bonanno

"She said 'fuck this shit', and she lived happily ever after."

– Anonymous

"I just want to live happily ever after, every now and then."
– Jimmy Buffett

Contradiction Alert!
"Happily ever after is so once upon a time."
– Anonymous

"There is no happily ever after to run to. We have to work for happiness."
– Mary Balogh

"And will I tell you that these three lived happily ever after?
I will not, for no one ever does. But there was happiness. And they did live."
– Stephen King

Happiness

"Do the things that make you happy, and don't do the things that make you sad."

– Captain Obvious (Tom Weber)

"Whoever said money can't buy happiness didn't know where to shop."

– Anonymous

"Happiness consists in realizing that it is all a great strange dream."

– Jack Kerouac

"A happy demeanor is a self-fulfilling prophecy."

– Sare Yogev

Retirement won't automatically bring happiness. If you weren't happy before your retirement, you may not be happy during retirement. Make some positive changes.

"When I'm weary… I ask my dead friends for their opinion and the answer is 'Whatever leads to joy'."

– Marie Howe

"Why do people spend their time being sad when they could be happy?"

– Andy Warhol

"You can't be sad when you're holding a cupcake."

– Button

"Do stuff you will enjoy thinking about and telling stories about for many years to come. Do stuff you will want to brag about."

– Rachel Maddow

"No medicine cures what happiness cannot."

– Gabriel Garci'a Ma'rquez

"Cherish all your happy moments; they make a fine cushion for old age."

– Booth Tarkington

"Happy memories never wear out."

– Joyce Beauregard

"The secret of happiness is to count your blessings and not your birthdays."

– Shannon Rose

"It's important to have a twinkle in your wrinkle."

– Anonymous

Happiness

"Do things that make you happy within the confines of the legal system."
– Ellen DeGeneres

"Imagine that you are on your death bed, then ask yourself: 'Am I happy with the life I led?' If 'not'—now is the time to make some positive changes."
– Tom Weber

"You can't make everyone happy… you are not a taco."
– Bumper Sticker

"Happiness is not necessarily the goal of life. Simple contentment being fine with your circumstances, is better than happiness."
– Dr. Andrew Weil

"Happiness is a by-product of an effort to make someone else happy."
– Greta Palmer

Hygge (hue-guh) is a Danish word for the feeling of contentedness, comfort, simpleness, and happiness created by a good moment. For example: sipping a cup of tea, sitting by a warm fire, wearing your favorite clothes, lounging on a cozy chair, and talking with good friends.

"Happiness? That's nothing more than health and a poor memory."
– Albert Schweitzer

"Pretend you are happy, and eventually you'll forget you're pretending."
– Reddit

Contradiction Alert!
"If only we'd stop trying to be happy we'd have a pretty good time."
– Edith Wharton

"Happiness is not on my list of priorities. I just deal with day-to-day things. If I'm happy—and if I'm not, I don't know the difference."
– Bob Dylan

Health

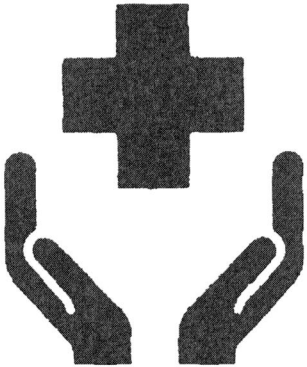

"He who has health has hope; and he who has hope has everything."
– Arabian Proverb

"The only way to keep your health is to eat what you don't want, drink what you don't like, and do what you'd rather not."
– Mark Twain

"Remember, being healthy is basically dying as slowly as possible."
– Ricky Gervais

"It's no longer a question of staying healthy. It's a question of finding a sickness you like."
– Jackie Mason

"Now that I've become a senior, everything's starting to click for me! My knees, my back, my neck…"
– Anonymous

"Let's drink to our health-plan!"
– Anonymous

"At my age getting a second doctor's opinion is kind of like switching slot machines."

– Jimmy Carter

"Live clean, think clean, and don't go to burlesque shows."

– Charles Atlas

"Obsessing over health is not healthy."

– Ashton Applewhite

"Birthdays are good for your health. Studies have shown that people who have more birthdays live the longest."
– Tumblr

Contradiction Alert!
"I knew a man who gave up smoking, drinking, sex and food. He was healthy right up to the time he killed himself."
– Johnny Carson

Hobbies

"You need to make good health a hobby."

– Jack LaLanne

"When a habit begins to cost money, it's called a hobby."

– Jewish Proverb

Go to a local craft shop to search for a hobby. Ask a clerk for advice and suggestions.

Renew an old interest.

"My hobby: listening to the same songs I've been listening to for over 20 years."

– Iain Morland

"Collect sunsets."

– Tom Weber

Develop a hobby with your spouse or partner.

"Sometimes your hobby can transform into a 'jobby'—an encore job."
– Anonymous

Identity

"What will you do now that you are done doing what you did?"
– Poster

"You *were* not just an employee, and you *are* now not just a retiree."
– Tom Weber

"Don't confuse what you do, with who you really are."
– Robert Laura

"I don't know who I am right now. But I know who I'm not. And I like that."
– Amber Smith

What do you want to be now that you're grown up? Identify your new identity. It will solidify with time. Then be proud and embrace it.

"The trouble is, when a number—your age—becomes your identity; you've given away your power to choose your future."
– Richard Leider

"What matters most is not 'what' you are, but 'who' you are."
– DaShanne Stokes

"It isn't where you came from—it's where you are going those counts."
– Ella Fitzgerald

"Follow your own compass."
– Tom Weber

"It's never too late to be what you might have been."
– George Eliot

"Imagine what you would put on a retirement business card: gardener, world traveler, golfer, reader."
– Tom Weber

Indulgence

"I must retire now to my couch of perpetual indulgence."
— George Miller

Splurge! Indulge your secret yearnings. Treat yourself, and spoil your spouse or partner.

"The more you weigh, the harder you are to kidnap. Stay safe. Eat cake."
— Anonymous

"The only time to eat diet food is while you're waiting for your steak to cook."
— Julia Child

"Never economize on luxuries."
— Angela Thirkell

"The senior citizen discount at the all-you-can-eat pizza smorgasbord."
— Dave Weber

"Nothing says indulgence in retirement…
    —like attending a matinee on a weekday.
    —like getting room service on a vacation.
    —like drinking the first cup of coffee in bed."

– Tom Weber

"If you can't be self-indulgent during retirement, then when can you be?"
– Tom Weber

Join Up

Join a club: a health club, a book club, a chess club…

Join an organization: The Red Hat Society, R.O.M.E.O. (Retired Old Men Eating Out), Cyber-Seniors…

Join Seniors Coalition, American Senior Association, your local senior center, American Association of Retired Persons (AARP)…

Join a team: bowling team, darts team, horseshoe team, pickle ball team…

Join a class: dance class, self-defense class, art class, yoga class…

Look up the online organization www.meetup.com to find nearby groups doing a variety of activities.

Laughter

"Humor greases the skids of life."

– Anonymous

"If you're not in the obits, eat breakfast."

– Carl Reiner

"With mirth and laughter let old wrinkles come."

– William Shakespeare

"I know not all that may be coming, but be it what it will, I'll go to it laughing."

– Herman Melville

"A good laugh overcomes more difficulties and dissipates more dark clouds than any other one thing."

– Laura Ingalls Wilder

"A good laugh and a long sleep are the two best cures for anything."

– Anonymous

"Laughter is the best medicine. Unless you have diarrhea."

— Anonymous

"I just want to spend the rest of my life laughing."

— Button

"A laugh is a smile that bursts."

— Mary H. Waldrip

"Laughter is a very underrated tool for healing."

— Bronnie Ware

"Life's burdens are lighter when I laugh at myself."

— Jonathan Lockwood Huie

"Old age? I'm only in it of the laughs."

— Leon Uris

"The best thing about retirement is not having to wear pants."

— Mark Hewer

"Retirement is all shits and giggles until someone giggles and shits."

— Anonymous

Lifelong Learning

"Always keep searching for 'aha!' moments."

— Tom Weber

Increase your retirement literacy. Make it your business to study and research the retirement lifestyle and its realities. Become a retirement scholar.

"As long as you live, keep learning how to live."

— Lucius Annaeus Seneca

Audit college classes. Most colleges allow retirees to take classes for free or at a greatly reduced rate. This means you can participate in the class, but no tests, no grades, and no pressure.

"Never use age as an excuse. You can teach an old dog new tricks."

— Tom Weber

Be a non-traditional student with 'Distance Learning'. Learn via Ted Talks, Podcasts, YouTube, and online college classes.

"Feed your head."

— Grace Slick

Learn a new skill: beer making, water color painting, piano, wood carving, calligraphy.

"By the time you're eighty years old, you've learned everything. You only have to remember it."

— George Burns

"Knowledge is like underwear. It is useful to have it, but not necessary to show it off."

– Bill Murray

"The length of your education is less important than its breadth, and the length of your life is less important than its depth."

– Marilyn Vos Savant

"Anyone who stops learning is old, whether at twenty or eighty. Anyone who keeps learning stays young."

– Henry Ford

"Travel is rich with learning opportunities, and the ultimate souvenir is a broader perspective."

– Rick Steves

"Use your noodle not the Google."
– Tom Weber

Legacy

"The things you do for yourself are gone when you are gone. The things you do for others remain as your legacy."

– Anonymous

"We may not be able to witness our own eulogy; but we're actually writing it all the time, every day."

– Arianna Huffington

"The greatest legacy you can leave your children is happy memories."

– Anonymous

"Die when I may, I want it said of me by those who know me best, that I have always plucked a thistle and planted a flower where I thought a flower would grow."

– Abraham Lincoln

"Let love be your legacy."

– Tom Weber

"Carve your name on hearts, not tombstones. A legacy is etched into the minds of others and the stories they share about you."

– Shannon Adler

"Live the way you want to be remembered."

– Anonymous

Life

"Some of the best days of your life haven't happened yet."
— Steven Aitchison

"When something goes wrong in your life, just yell 'Plot Twist!' and move on."
— Meme

"In the book of life, the answers aren't in the back."
— Charles Schultz

"We have two lives, and the second begins when we realize we only have one."
— Confucius

"Life is uncertain. Eat dessert first."
— Ernestine Ulmer

"Life does not have to be perfect to be wonderful."
— Annette Funicello

"Ob-la-di ob-la-da life goes on bra La-la-la how life goes on."
— Paul McCartney and John Lennon

"Live so that the preacher won't have to lie at your funeral."
— Anonymous

"You only live once, but if you do it right, once is enough."
— Mae West

"If you're not in the parade, you watch the parade. That's life."
— Mike Ditka

"Life is short—avoid causing yawns."

– Elinor Glyn

"Not a shred of evidence exists in favor of the idea that life is serious."

– Brendan Gill

"Life is too short to worry about how short life is."

– Bumper Sticker

"To succeed in life, you need three things: a wishbone, a backbone, and a funny bone."

– Reba McIntire

"Enjoy every sandwich."

– Warren Zevon

"Life is a great big canvas, and you should throw all the paint on it you can."

– Danny Kaye

"When you get to my age, life seems little more than one long march to and from the lavatory."

– John Mortimer

"Life is a wheel of fortune and it's my turn to spin it."

– Tupac Shakur

"Life always begins with one step outside of your comfort zone."

– Shannon L. Alder

"Life is a hell of a lot more fun if you say yes rather than no."
– Richard Branson

Note: Insert the word "Retirement" for the word "Life" and re-read this page.

Longevity

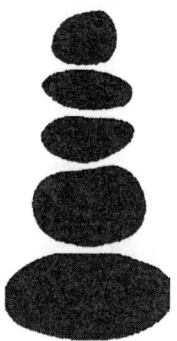

"The secret to a long life is to keep on breathing."

– Willie Nelson

"Live long and prosper."

– Mr. Spock: from "Star Trek"

"Life expectancy would grow by leaps and bounds if green vegetables smelled as good as bacon."

– Doug Larson

"Wish not so much to live long as to live well."

– Ben Franklin

"To sustain longevity, you have to evolve."

– Aries Spears

"You do what you can for as long as you can, and when you finally can't, you do the next best thing."

– Chuck Yeager

"To avoid sickness, eat less; to prolong life worry less."

– Chu Hui Weng

"Key to longevity…drinking embalming fluid every year."
– Angus Young

"The goal is to stay healthy, not stay young. Longevity is a bonus."
– Ashton Applewhite

"I intend to live forever. So far, so good."
– Steven Wright

"One of the secrets of a long and fruitful life is to forgive everybody everything every night before you go to bed."
– Anonymous

"You can't do anything about the length of your life, but you can do something about its width and depth."
– H. L. Mencken

"You can live to be 100 if you give up all the things that make you want to live to be 100."
– Woody Allen

Contradiction Alert!
"The quality, not the longevity, of one's life is what's important."
– Martin Luther King Jr.

"If the purpose of life is just to prolong your life, then maybe there's not much life to prolong."
– Stephan Pastis

Looks

"It's great to have gray hair. Ask anyone who's bald."
— Anonymous

"How do I stay so healthy and boyishly handsome? It's simple. I drink the blood of young runaways."
— William Shatner

"Remember that wrinkles merely indicate where smiles have been."
— Mark Twain

"You can only hold your stomach in for so many years."
— Burt Reynolds

"The best way to keep looking young is to hang out with older people."
— Anonymous

"If I'd known I was going to live this long I would have taken better care of myself."
— Eubie Blake

"Nothing is more beautiful than cheerfulness in an old face."
— Jean Paul Richter

"Everyone looks so much better when they smile."
— Jimmy Fallon

"Careful grooming may take 20 years off a woman's age, but you can't fool a flight of stairs."
— Marlene Dietrich

"Old people who shine from the inside look 10 to 20 years younger."
– Dolly Parton

"Being young is beautiful, but being old is comfortable."
– Marie Ebner—Eisenbach

"My inner child doesn't recognize the outer elder in the mirror."
– Tom Weber

"Maybe you should eat some makeup so you can be pretty on the inside too."
– Mitch Hedberg

"I'm glad wrinkles don't hurt."
– Anonymous

"Whatever wrinkles I got, I enjoyed getting them."
– Ava Gardner

"Time marches on and sooner or later you realize it is marching across your face."
– Robert Harling

"When nine hundred years old you reach, look as good you will not."
– Yoda

"Time can be a great healer, but a lousy beautician."
– Anonymous

Contradiction Alert!
"Inner beauty is great, but a little mascara never hurt."
– Tumblr

Love

"A heart that loves is always young."

– Proverb

"True love isn't Romeo and Juliet who died together, it's grandma and grandpa who grew old together."

– Tumblr

"Surround yourself with what you love."

– George Carlin

"Love is not having to hold your farts in anymore."

– Anonymous

"People should fall in love with their eyes closed."

– Andy Warhol

"That love thy neighbor stuff? I meant that."

– God

"And in the end the love you take is equal to the love you make."
– John Lennon and Paul McCartney

"You are never too old or too broken to be in love."
– Tumblr

Marriage

"Grow old with me. The best is yet to be."

– Robert Browning

"I wanna make you smile whenever you're sad
Carry you around when your arthritis is bad
All I wanna do is grow old with you."

– Adam Sandler

"The love we have in our youth is superfluous compared to the love that an old man has for his wife."

– Will Durant

"Your marriage in retirement will be blissful if you have open and honest communication, provide each other with emotional support, and tolerate each other's idiosyncrasies."

– Sara Yogev

You and your spouse or partner will experience the transition to retirement differently. Sync up every aspect of your retirement with each other. Have an expectation exchange. Articulate expectations, dreams, and visions of retirement, so that you can achieve them together. And while you're at it, renegotiate old and create new marital and domestic ground rules.

"Give each other physical and emotional space."

– Sara Yogev

Create a balance between your independent individuality and interdependent togetherness. Develop three distinct worlds: My World, Your World, and Our World.

"Let there be spaces in your togetherness."

– Kahlil Gibran

"An archaeologist is the best husband any woman can have; the older she gets, the more interested he is in her."

– Agatha Christie

"For better or worse—but not all day."

– Cheryl Hanson

"The 4 dreaded words in any retirement marriage: 'I'll go with you'."

– Anonymous

"Get used to a spouse around the house."
– Refrigerator Magnet

Memory

Exercise your aging mind with card games and word puzzles. Play the games against the clock to make them even more mentally challenging.

Up the mental difficulty of an activity and up the positive results. Learn a new language, take up a new musical instrument, or try some new technology.

"God gave us memories so that we might have roses in December."
– James M. Barrie

"A good life is a collection of happy memories."
– Denis Waitley

"Cherish all your happy moments; they make a fine cushion for old age."
– Booth Tarkington

"I have a date with a memory."
– Humphrey Bogart

"The older I get—the better I was."
– Anonymous

"Not only is my short-term memory horrible, but so is my short-term memory."
– Tumblr

"I want to visit Memory Lane; I don't want to live there."

– Letty Cottin

"Sometimes a short walk down Memory Lane is all it takes to appreciate where you are today."

– Susan Gale

"Old photographs fuel a trip down Memory Lane."

– Anonymous

"Every man's memory is his private literature."

– Aldous Huxley

"You're not senile. You're 'Retiremental!'"
– Tom Weber

Contradiction Alert!
"There are times when forgetting can be as important as remembering—and even more difficult."
– Harry Mier

Mindfulness

"Mindfulness means being awake. It means knowing what you are doing."
– Jon Kabat-Zinn

"The best way to capture moments is to pay attention. This is how we cultivate mindfulness."
– Jon Kabat-Zinn

"Being mindful means that we suspend judgment for a time, set aside our immediate goals for the future, and take in the present moment as it is rather than as we would like it to be."
– Mark Williams

"If we knew that tonight we were going to go blind, we would take a longing, last real look at every blade of grass, every cloud formation, every speck of dust, every rainbow, raindrop—everything."
– Perna Chadron

"The little things? The little moments? They aren't little."
– Jon Kabat-Zinn

"Do not dwell in the past, do not dream of the future, concentrate the mind on the present moment."
– Buddha

"There's a difference between mind filling and mindful activities."
— Tom Weber

Be a 'Nowist', a person who believes in living in the moment.

"Learning to ignore things is one of the great paths to inner peace."
— Robert Sawyer

"Life is a dance. Mindfulness is witnessing that dance."
— Amit Ray

"Paying attention on purpose, in the present moment, and non-judgmentally."
— Jon Kabat-Zinn

"Live the actual moment. Only this actual moment is life."
— Thich Nha't Hmh

"Wherever you are, be there totally."
— Eckhart Tolle

"Begin within!"
— Bumper Sticker

Moderation

"Small helpings. Sample a little bit of everything. These are the secrets of happiness and good health. You need to enjoy the good things in life, but you need not overindulge."
– Julia Child

"Moderation in all things, especially moderation."
– Ralph Waldo Emerson

"I'll live longer, with a better quality of life, if I eat well, but that doesn't mean I shouldn't enjoy a bucket of KFC and a candy bar once in a while."
– Steven Petrow

"One man's moderation is another man's revelry."
– Anonymous

"If one oversteps the bounds of moderation, the greatest pleasures cease to please."
– Anonymous

"I am good, but not an angel. I do sin, but I am not the devil."
– Anonymous

"No physical appearance is worth not eating pasta for."
– Bumper Sticker

"Everything in moderation—except bacon."
– Bumper Sticker

"Everything in moderation, especially this inspirational bullshit."
– Anonymous

Contradiction Alert!
"Moderation is a fatal thing. Nothing succeeds like excess."
– Oscar Wilde

Money

"It is better to live rich than to die rich."

– Samuel Johnson

"Retirement Resolution: Never discount senior discounts."

– Tom Weber

"Money is not everything, according to those who have it."

– Malcolm Forbes

"I'm worried that I didn't save enough money for retirement alcohol."

– Anonymous

"Money is a terrible master, but an excellent servant."

– P. T Barnum

"Figure out the relationship between money and happiness."

– Wes Moss

"Maybe money can't buy happiness, but I think it's only fair to give me some and let me learn that lesson myself."

– Iain Morland

"'Dough Phobia' is the abnormal fear of outliving your money."

– Anonymous

"It's nice to get out of the rat race, but you have to learn to get along with less cheese."

– Gene Perret

"Stuck between 'I need to save money' and 'You only live once'."

– Iain Morland

"The things I buy now will never wear out."

– Art Linkletter

"Why is there so much month left at the end of the money."

– Lionel Barrymore

Retirement is more than a math problem regarding your money. Don't be cash rich and lifestyle poor.

"Retirement is like a long vacation in Las Vegas. The goal is to enjoy it the fullest, but not so fully that you run out of money."

– Jonathan Clemens

"Running out of money pales in comparison to running out of family, friends, good health, and time."
– Robert Laura

Contradiction Alert!
"Some people are so poor, all they have is money."
– Graffiti

Motivation

"Do not go gentle into that good night—rage, rage against the dying of the light."

— Dylan Thomas

"Find a quote or create a motto that will motivate you throughout your retirement. Write it down, and put it on your refrigerator as a reminder."

— Sue Weber

"Don't retire. Inspire!"

— Mickey Rooney

"You didn't come this far to only come this far."

— Tumblr

"When life knocks you down, stand up and say, 'You hit like a bitch'."

— Iain Morland

"Retirement Resolution: Never say die!"
– Tom Weber

"You can't wait for inspiration. You have to go after it with a club."
– Jack London

"And the world will be better for this
That one man, scorned and covered with scars,
Still strove with his last ounce of courage
To reach the unreachable star."
– Joe Darion

"Aspire to inspire before you expire!"
– Bumper Sticker

"If you need motivation – just visit a cemetery."
– Tom Weber

Music

"Without music life is a journey through a desert."

– Pat Conroy

Create a sound track for your life. Keep music playing, in the background, throughout the day.

"Karaoke like nobody's listening."

– Bumper Sticker

Dust off your old instrument from your high school band days and play away.

"The secret is to listen to more music and less advice."

– Anonymous

"Don't sing in the shower—perform!"

– Tumblr

"One good thing about music, when it hits you, you feel no pain."

– Bob Marley

"Bring out the old vinyls. It's like getting in touch with old friends."

– Anonymous

"Slow down and smell Guns N' Roses."

– Anonymous

"The older the violin, the sweeter the music."

– Larry McMurtry

"One old song. A thousand old memories."
– Tumblr

Naps

"Taking naps sounds so childish. I prefer to call them horizontal life pauses."
— Anonymous

"You know you're old when happy hour is a nap."
— Bumper Sticker

"Go mocking!" (Napping in a hammock)
— Dave Ziebarth

"Retirement Resolution: Never decline to recline!"
— Tom Weber

"Naps prevent aging—especially if you take them while driving."
— Button

"No day is so bad it can't be fixed with a nap."
— Carrie P. Snow

"May we learn to honor the hammock, the siesta, the nap, and the pause in all its forms."
— Alice Walker

"Take a 'Nano Nap'. Little naps lead to big benefits."
— Tom Weber

"I enjoy waking up and not having to go to work. So I do it three or four times a day."

— Anonymous

"To keep going, we sometimes need to allow ourselves to stop."

– Gretchen Rubin

"Figure out what to do, then take a nap."

– Adam Carolla

"Ah napping…or as I like to call it…pressing life's pause button."

– Garfield (by Jim Davis)

"I never drink coffee at lunch. I find it keeps me awake for the afternoon."

– Ronald Regan

"Siesta Time! How can the entire Spanish culture be wrong."

– Tom Weber

"Take a 20 minute nap, and wake up 2 hours later."
– Anonymous

Nature

"Think outside. No box required."

— Billboard

"Step outside for a while—calm your mind. It is better to hug a tree than to bang your head against a wall continually."

— Rasheed Ogunlaru

"I see skies of blue and clouds of white
The bright blessed day, the dark sacred night
And I think to myself what a wonderful world."

— Louis Daniel Armstrong

"Nature is not a place to visit. It is home."

— Gary Snyder

"The woods are like my church."

— Shug

Enjoy the many positive benefits of a Japanese "Forest Bath".

"Bring nature inside. Keep a vase of fresh flowers in your home."

— Sue Weber

"Fresh air impoverishes the doctor."

— Danish Proverb

"Sit still until you disappear. Then experience what the world is like without you."

— Anonymous

"May the forest be with you."
– Bumper Sticker

"Surely, of all the wonders of the world, the horizon is the greatest."
– Freya Stark

"Grab a pair of binoculars and hike with your eyes."
– Steve Weber

"Connect with nature. Sit on a park bench in a natural setting and just absorb the influence of the place."
– Andrew Weil

"Look around. Look at what we have. Beauty is everywhere – you only have to look to see it."
– Bob Ross

Nostalgia

"Nostalgia ain't what it used to be."

– Peter DeVries

"Nostalgia is like sex. Every generation thinks it's discovering it for the first time."

– Michael Barrier

"Advice is a form of nostalgia."

– Mary Schmich

"Songs instigate nostalgia."

– Anonymous

"I prefer the mystic clouds of nostalgia to the real thing, to be honest."

– Robert Wyatt

"Sometimes you heat things up on the stove instead of in the microwave, just to be nostalgic."

– Anonymous

"Nostalgia is heroin for old people."
– Dara O'Brian

"What's wrong with a bit of nostalgia between friends? I think nostalgia sometimes gets too much of a bad press."

– Terry Eagleton

"Nostalgia: a device that removes the ruts and potholes from Memory Lane."
– Doug Larson

Contradiction Alert!
"I don't do nostalgia. It just doesn't occur to me. I'm living in the moment, and I don't have that gene."
– Harrison Ford

Old

"Being old doesn't seem so old now that I'm old."
– Bumper Sticker

"You're not as young as you used to be. But you're not as old as you're going to be."
– Irish Saying

"Every day I understand the phrase 'I'm getting too old for this shit' on an even deeper level."
– Iain Morland

"You're only old once."
– Dr. Seuss

"Every man desire to live long, but no man desires to be old."
– Jonathan Swift

"You can't help getting older, but you don't have to get old."
– George Burns

"It is not how old you are, but how you are old."
– Marie Dressler

"To me old age is always 15 years older than I am."
– Bernard Baruch

"You can get old pretty young if you don't take care of yourself."
– Yogi Berra

"One great thing about getting old is that you can get out of all sorts of social obligations just by saying you're too tired."
– George Carlin

"I thought growing old would take longer."
– Button

"How old would you be if you didn't know how old you was?"
– Satchel Page

**"You know you are old
when you see your childhood toys in the antique store."**
– Anonymous

Old

"You're too young to be old."

– Nancy Schlossberg

"Growing old is something you do if you're lucky."

– Groucho Marx

"I never let the old man in."

– Clint Eastwood

"Old age and treachery will always beat youth and exuberance."

– Anonymous

"A man is not old as long as he is seeking something."

– Jean Rostand

"The older you get, the older you want to get."

– Keith Richards

"I can't wait until I'm old enough to pretend I can't hear."

– Iain Morland

"Many men die at twenty-five and aren't buried until they are seventy-five."

– Benjamin Franklin

"Old age is not for sissies."

Betty Davis

"Age appears to be best in four things; old wood to burn, old wine to drink, old friends to trust, and old authors to read."

– Francis Bacon

"Old age isn't so bad when you consider the alternative."

– Maurice Chevalier

"The older I get, the better I used to be."

– Lee Trevino

"We are not limited by our old age; we are liberated by it."

– Stu Mittleman

"I hate it when I see some old person and then realize we went to high school together."

– Anonymous

"Growing old is compulsory—growing up is optional."

– Bob Monkhouse

"You're only old—when you think you are."

– Anonymous

"Age and glasses of wine should never be counted."

– Anonymous

"We should start referring to 'age' as 'levels', so when you're LVL 80 it sounds more badass."

– Anonymous

"Old people are just young people who have been alive for a very long time."

– Anonymous

"You can still be a kid…even when you're old."
– Dennis the Menace

I'm Not Old (Compared to Fossils). I'm…

- Chronologically gifted!
- Upper middle-age!
- Vintage!
- Of a certain age!
- Mature!
- 55 plus shipping and handling!
- Numerically endowed!
- Evolving!
- Young for a very long time!
- Retro!
- A recycled teenager!
- Classic!
- Young enough to remember when Pluto was a planet!
- Afflicted with senior-itis!
- On the right side of 65!
- Seasoned

I'm Not Retired. I'm…

- A recovering workaholic!
- An employee escapee!
- The 'R' word!
- On permanent sabbatical!
- An unemployment volunteer!
- Gainfully unemployed!
- A work refugee!

Optimism

"Dear Optimist, Pessimist, and Realist,
While you guys were arguing about the glass of water being half full or half empty. I drank it."
— The Opportunist

"You can't look at a glass half full or empty if it's overflowing."
— Kanye West

"People waste their time pondering whether a glass is half empty or half full. Me, I just drink whatever's in the glass."
— Sophia: from 'The Golden Girls'

"Fairy tales can come true.
They can happen to you.
If you're young at heart."
— Johnny Richards and Carolyn Leigh

"The barn burned down. Now I can see the moon."
— Zen Saying

"Everything will be okay in the end. If it's not okay it's not the end."
— Ed Sheeran

"I have never seen a monument erected to a pessimist."

– Paul Harvey

"Be a warrior for optimism."

– Cameron Crow

"Positive attitudes about retirement, the future, and aging in general facilitate the adjustment to retirement."

– Sara Yogev

"An optimist is someone who goes after Moby Dick in a rowboat and takes the tartar sauce with him."

– Zig Ziglar

Pastimes

Golf

"Retirement means no pressure, no stress, no heartache—unless you play golf."

– Gene Perret

"Don't play too much golf. Three rounds a day is enough."

– Harry Vardon

Fishing

I didn't retire. I became a professional fisherman.

– Refrigerator Magnet

"Good things come to those who bait."

– Bumper Sticker

Gardening

"Gardening is better than therapy. And you get tomatoes."

– Anonymous

"Grow your garden. Grow your health."

– Anonymous

Peace

"I have learned to read the papers calmly and not to hate the fools I read about."
– Edmund Wilson

"Learning to ignore things is one of the great paths to inner peace."
– Meme

"Take a moment every day to find peace. Pull over to the side of the road, turn off the radio, and find peace."
– Richard Simmons

"The competition is over. You can relax. You've made your life what it is and you no longer need to prove yourself. You can relax and enjoy whatever degree of involvement you want."
– Stansfield Turner

"Serenity now. Serenity now. Calm blue ocean. Calm blue ocean."
– Mantras from "Seinfeld"

"Increase the peace!"
– Ali G

Physical Activity

"Physically active on a regular, permanent basis can help prevent or delay certain diseases (like some types of cancer, heart disease, or diabetes) and disabilities as people grow older."
– Dr. Andrew Weil

"The biggest sin is sitting on your ass."
– Florynce Kennedy

"Life is like riding a bicycle. To keep your balance, you must keep moving."

– Albert Einstein

"Don't burden yourself by making your life too easy."

– Anonymous

Doing physical tasks around the house and in the yard are a form of exercise. Trim hedges. Climb stairs. Rake leaves. Vacuum carpets. Mow lawn.

"Leave an impression on the world—not the couch."
– Anonymous

Pets

A pet's love and companionship fills emptiness and stimulates your lifestyle.

"Dog walks are good for the soul."
— Bumper Sticker

"Our perfect companions never have fewer than four feet."
— Colette

"If your dog is fat, you're not getting enough exercise."
— Tee Shirt

"Find your next best friend at the animal shelter."
— Bumper Sticker

Pet people are the nicest people. Make new friends at the dog park or at the pet store.

"Time spent with cats is never wasted."
— Sigmund Freud

Petting a pet is linked to lowering blood pressure and stress levels.

"Anyone who doesn't think you can buy love,
has never visited a pet store."
– Anonymous

Play

"Men do not quit playing because they grow old; they grow old because they quit playing."
– Oliver Wendell Holmes

"Play is our brain's favorite way of learning."
– Diane Ackerman

"Play without purpose. Remember the joy you had at recess in school!"
– Tom Weber

Not that you need justification, but you worked hard, so now you can play hard.

"The opposite of play is not work. It's depression."
– Brian Sutton-Smith

"When you're done with your chores, then you can go out and play."
– Joyce Weber: My Mom

"Create a 'Play Jar'. Just like a 'Job Jar', but different."
– Tom Weber

Procrastination

"There are only so many 'some days' left."
— Traveler on the Alaskan Highway

"It's gotten to the point where I can't even call what I'm doing procrastinating anymore. I should just be calling it jeopardizing my future."
— Author Unknown

"Someday (Someday I'll do this. Someday I'll do that.) is a disease that will take your dreams to the grave with you. Procrastination is the art of keeping up with yesterday."
— Don Marquis

"My mother always told me I wouldn't amount to anything because I procrastinate. I said, 'Just wait'."
— Judy Tenuta

"It is very important what not to do."
— Iggy Pop

"How soon 'not now' becomes 'never'."
— Martin Luther

"Procrastinator? No. I just wait until the last second to do my work because I will be older, therefore wiser."
— Tumblr

"I'm taking care of my procrastination issues; just you wait and see."
— Anonymous

"Get off your leash, and sniff out some of life's wag your tail moments."
— Tom Weber

"Dost thou love life? Then do not squander time, for that is the stuff life is made of."

– Poor Richard

"A day can really slip by when you're deliberately avoiding what you're supposed to do."

– Bill Waters

"It is never too late. Just as it is never too early."

– Fortune Cookie

"Everyone who is taken by death asks for more time, while everyone who still has time makes excuses for procrastination."

– Ali ibn e Abi Talib

"Do not lead a '3D' Life of Delay, Defer, and Deprive."
– Tom Weber

Contradiction Alert!
"Procrastinate like there's no tomorrow."
– Anonymous

"Procrastinate now, don't put it off."
– Ellen DeGeneres

Purpose

"Have a reason for getting up each morning."
– Retiree in café

"Don't simply retire from something; have something to retire to."
– Harry Emerson Fosdick

"No alarm clock needed. My passion wakes me!"
– Poster

"The purpose of life, after all, is to live it, to taste experience to the utmost, to reach out eagerly and without fear for newer and richer experiences."
– Eleanor Roosevelt

"Follow your passion. It will lead you to your purpose."
– Oprah Winfrey

"Passion before purpose."
– Kathy Gilbride

"Don't count your days. Make your days count."
– Rev. Billy Graham

Pursue highly engaging, challenging, complex, and fun activities.

"Your sense of purpose is worth up to 7 years of extra life expectancy."
– Dan Buettner

"Tell me, what is it you plan to do with your one wild and precious life?"
– Mary Oliver

Contradiction Alert!
"Cats are intended to teach us that not everything in nature has a purpose."
– Garrison Keillor

"Listen: we are here on earth to fart around.
Don't let anyone tell you different."
– Kurt Vonnegut

"My life has no purpose, no direction, no aim, no meaning, and yet I'm happy. I can't figure it out. What am I doing right?"
– Charles Schultz

Quality of Life

"Life is too short to drink cheap wine."

– Refrigerator Magnet

"Life is not measured by the number of breaths we take, but by the places and moments that take our breath away."

– George Carlin

"Invest your life. Don't just spend it."

– Rev. Billy Graham

"It's all about quality of life and finding a happy balance."

– Philip Green

"Don't live the same year 75 times and call it life."
– Robin Sharma

Questions

Imagine you are at a gathering and a someone approaches you and asks…

"How do you like retirement?"
"Do you miss work?"
"What do you do all day?"

Will you be ready to respond?

Regrets

"Regret for wasted time is more wasted time."
— Mason Cooley

"Do not regret what you aren't. Find joy in what you are."
— Anonymous

"Never regret. If it's good, it's wonderful. If it's bad, it's experience."
— Victoria Holt

"Fear regret more than failure."
— Taryn Rose

Every life has its misfortunes. Try not to dwell on them.

"You are old when regrets take the place of dreams."

– Anonymous

"Woulda, shoulda, and coulda is no gooda."
– Tom Weber

Relaxation

"Aging can be fun if you lay back and enjoy it."

– Clint Eastwood

"Sometimes the most productive thing you can do is relax."

– Mark Black

"For retirement brings repose (rest and tranquility), and repose allows a kindly judgment of all things."

– John Sharp Williams

"Max relax! Dress to chill: slippers, pajamas, and robe."

– Tom Weber

"There must be quite a few things that a hot bath won't cure, but I don't know many of them."

– Sylvia Plath

"Don't lean in! Lean back!"
– Tom Weber

Retirement

"Carpe emeritus! = Seize your retirement!"

– Tom Weber

"The greatest potential for growth and self-realization exists in the second half of life."

– Carl Yung

"Y.O.L.O. = You Only Live Once! Y.O.R.O. = You Only Retire Once!"

– Tom Weber

You are responsible for the quality of your retirement. You must personalize and customize your retirement for whatever you feel is natural, important, and satisfying.

Prepare for a long retirement. With longevity climbing, your retirement could easily last 20 to 30 years or more. It's a marathon not a sprint. Have a realistic view of retirement. Don't idealize it. It's not all vacations and holidays.

"I like retirement—it's the best job I ever had."

– Mike Stuber

"My retirement plan is to get thrown into a minimum-security prison in Hawaii."

– Julius Sharpe

"Retirement is the Promised Land, but remember even Moses struggled sometimes in the Promised Land."

– Tom Weber

"Retire from work, but not from life."

– M. K. Soni

"In retirement, every day is 'Tom Weber Appreciation Day'—and I'm Tom Weber!"

– Tom Weber

"It is time I stepped aside for a less experienced and less able man."

– Scott Elledge

"Retirement: the pay sucks, but the hours are good."

– Refrigerator Magnet

"Often when you think you're at the end of something you're at the beginning of something else."

– Mister Rogers

Re-Retire

If ***Retiremental!*** has given you a fresh outlook regarding retirement, then feel free to 'Re-Retire'. No matter what stage of retirement you are in restart your retirement with a new and improved attitude and approach.

Retirement Adjustments

"Focus on what you can do, not what you can't."
– Anonymous

"Start where you are. Do what you can. Use what you have!"
– Anonymous

"As your life changes, it takes time to recalibrate, to find your values again. You might also find that retirement is the time when you stretch out and find your potential."
– Sid Miramontes

"If your plan isn't working, adjust your plan. Never give up."
– Matt Martin

Rather than give up a favorite activity—replace it with a creative substitute.

—Instead of tennis—badminton.

—Instead of badminton—ping pong.

—Instead of ping pong—Well, you get the idea.

"I adapt and I adjust to whatever environment I'm in."

– Kevin Gates

"You're never too old, and it's never too late."

– Marcia Muth

"Get the knack of getting people to help you and also pitch in yourself."

– Ruth Gordon

"Blessed are the flexible, for they shall not be bent out of shape."

– Anonymous

Retirement Celebration

Retirements, like graduations and weddings, are an important milestone is a person's life. Often this rite of passage is marked with some sort of dinner, party, or celebration. It's a time to acknowledge achievements and to say farewells. It will bring a sense of closure to your job as it bridges the gap to your next new phase of life.

Retirement Environment

"Create your own 'Shangri-La' in your own back yard."
— Tom Weber

Establish separate territories in your home for both you and your spouse.

Allocate special spaces in which to play, rest, and work.

"A comfortable house is a great source of happiness. It ranks immediately after health and good conscience."
— Sydney Smith

Create a home sanctuary that is free from the busyness and chaos of everyday life.

"No money is better spent than what is laid out for domestic satisfaction."
– Samuel Johnson

"He is the happiest, be he king or peasant, who finds peace in his home."
– Goethe

Retirement Goals

"A goal is not always meant to be reached, it often serves simply as something to aim at."

– Bruce Lee

"My goal this week is to move…just enough so people don't think I'm dead."

– Anonymous

"Age is just a number. Yes, our bodies do age and our appearance can change, however, some people start aging at a very young age. They are content to sit on a couch and not set any goals. Whereas, some older people never stop having goals."

– Catherine Pulsifer

"Know your goal, make a plan and pull the trigger."

– Dr. Phil

"Carry your most important goal in your wallet."

– Jack Canfield

"You can, you should, and if you're brave enough to start, you will."

– Stephen King

"You are never too old to set another goal or dream a new dream."
– C.S. Lewis

Contradiction Alert!
"Goals aren't as important as we think. Try working without them for a week. Turns out, you can do amazing things without goals. You're less stressed without goals, and you're freer to choose paths you couldn't have foreseen without them."
– Leo Babauta

Retirement: The Golden Years

Traditionally retirement was referred to as the Golden Years. It was a time for relaxation and leisure. Sleeping late, shuffle board, jig saw puzzles, and mounting photos in photo albums. Today this view, may still be practiced by some, but for many retirees the Golden Years have transformed into a more active and productive time of life.

"Others will keep working because the 'gold' in our so-called 'Golden Years' doesn't have to come from watching sunsets."
– Arianna Huffington

Contradiction Alert!
"The Golden Years have come at last.
The Golden Years can kiss my ass."
– Dr. Seuss

Retirement Guilt

You've earned and deserve a happy guilt-free retirement. If you feel retirement guilt for your friends who haven't retired yet—don't. Your empathy is admirable, but ultimately your retirement fate is in your hands and theirs is up to them. They will get their chance. Sooner or later we all retire, and sooner or later your retirement guilt will subside.

Retirement: Honeymoon

The first months of retirement are called the Honeymoon. With euphoric enthusiasm retirees enjoy the liberating novelty of early retirement. The Honeymoon is like a perpetual vacation filled with relaxation, leisure, and free time that retirees rarely enjoyed while they worked. It includes, but is not limited to, hiking, gardening, biking, reading, and traveling.

The Honeymoon is sometimes referred to as the Moneymoon because retirees are more concerned about having meaningful experiences than about running out of money. Pace yourself during the Honeymoon. Retirement is a long haul. Follow your plan and remember your budget. Many retirees give in to the urge to overspend during this Stage.

Retirement Mentors

Seek out a mentor to guide you along the retirement path.

Find a seasoned retiree, someone you respect and trust, who is willing to share helpful tips, offer insights, and answer questions.

"The delicate balance of mentoring someone is not creating them in your own image, but giving them the opportunity to create themselves."
— Steven Spielberg

A mentor will help you to achieve your potential in retirement.

Let the mentor/mentee relationship grow naturally and informally. Express your gratitude to your mentor.

"Mentoring is a brain to pick, an ear to listen, and a push in the right direction."
— John Crosby

Retirement Phases

When workers think about what retirement will be like, they often imagine it as a single huge event. In reality, retirement is three phases, and for most retirees each stage is considerably different.

"Go-Go" Retirement Phase

The **Go-Go Phase** is the active retirement phase. It is the early retirement phase when retirees tend to be physically and mentally capable of living a fairly active lifestyle. This phase may not be that much different than pre-retirement except that there is more time to do things like travel and hobbies. Because new retirees are relatively young, they're often in good health and have a relatively high energy level.

"Slow-Go" Retirement Phase

The **Slow-Go Phase** of retirement is a more stable and passive. Retirees are still active in this phase, but they've slowed down often due to lesser energy levels. They've done a lot of the things they'd planned for retirement, and though they're still traveling and pursing hobbies, they're also settling into comfortable routines and predictable patterns at home. This is a time when many retirees usually choose to focus on family activities.

"No-Go" Retirement Phase

The last phase of retirement is the **No-Go Phase**. In this phase, time and age play a role in slowing down many activities and abilities. Life undergoes significant changes sometimes mental, sometimes physical, and sometimes financial. Often this stage requires some level of support from family, government, or agencies.

Retirement Reading

"Always read something that will make you look good if you die in the middle of it."

– P.J. O'Rourke

"Reading is a discount ticket to everywhere."

– Mary Schmich

"A reader lives a thousand lives before he dies. The man who never reads lives only one."

– George R. Martin

"If we didn't have libraries, many people thirsty for knowledge would dehydrate."

– Meganjo Tetrick (age 12)

"No entertainment is so cheap as reading, nor any pleasure so lasting."
– Mary Wortley Montagu

"Reading is to the mind what exercise is to the body."

– Joseph Addison

"I was reading a book, 'The History of Glue', I couldn't put it down."

– Tim Vine

"I find television very educating. Every time somebody turns on the set, I go into the other room and read a book."

– Groucho Marx

"Let's be reasonable and add an eighth day to the week that is devoted exclusively to reading."

– Lena Dunham

"My wife joined a book club. They primarily read wine labels."

– Anonymous

"Literature is the most agreeable way of ignoring life."

– Fernando Pessoa

"Books are the blessed chloroform of the mind."
– Robert Chambers

Retirement Relevance

Continue interacting with the world. Keep current with: the latest technology, the latest news, and the latest styles. If you do not, you relegate yourself to being a remnant of the past.

Retirement Risk

"You gotta risk it to get the biscuit."
– Jimmy Fallon

"You got to be brave. If you feel something, you've really got to risk it."
– Mel Brooks

"Great deeds are usually wrought at great risks."
– Herodotus

"If no one ever took risks, Michelangelo would have painted the Sistine floor."
– Neil Simon

"Risks must be taken because the greatest hazard in life is to risk nothing."
– Leo F. Buscaglia

"Living at risk is jumping off the cliff and building your wings on the way down."
– Ray Bradbury

"Do one thing every day that scares you."
– Eleanor Roosevelt

"Go out on a limb—that's where the fruit is."
– Jimmy Carter

Retirement Robbers

A retirement robber keeps you from following your retirement dreams.

Retirement Robbers:

1. Being too busy.
2. Procrastination.
3. Fear.

Solutions:

1. Don't over commit. Learn to say 'No' thankfully, tactfully, and graciously.
2. Take control of your own time. Set boundaries based on what you want to do.
3. Adopt a fight, not flight, attitude.

Retirement Routine

Don't be List-less. Start each day with an informal to-do list or schedule. Experiment with your list or schedule as you discover the rhythm to your new normal.

"Custom-design your days, weeks, and months."
— Sara Yogev

You don't need to account for every hour of every day. Do not over-plan your life or plan too far in advance. Commit yourself to having a significant amount of unstructured free time every day. Leave room for spontaneity. Many highlights in life aren't planned. They just happen. Be flexible. It is difficult to predict all the opportunities that will be presented to you.

"Establishing new schedules and routines is a great way to make the transition into retirement easier and help seniors find a new path forward."
— Samantha Westwood

Regularly change up your routine. Stir up your physical, social, and intellectual activities.

"Variety is the spice of retirement."
— Tom Weber

"Don't prioritize your schedule. Schedule your priorities."
— Stephen R. Covey

Contradiction Alert!
Throw out the to-do list! Just do what you want when you want.

"The less of routine, the more of life."
— A.B. Alcott

Retirement Transition

From Employee to Retiree

"Get a good start in your retirement because: Well begun is half done."
– Anonymous

Retirement is not one transition, but many. Your success in retirement depends upon your ability to adjust, evaluate, and recalibrate. At first, you feel like a fish out of water, but eventually you acclimate.

"It can take as long as three years to completely adjust to your retirement. Be patient and know that a new life is awakening within you."
– Mark Evan Chomsky

"As you embark on the exciting journey into retirement, you will experience a transition that will be both thrilling and terrifying."
– Olivia Greenwell

"Change always comes bearing gifts."
– Price Pritchett

"Be a Savvy Senior. Create a 'Retirement Mission Statement' or a 'Retirement Manifesto'."

– Tom Weber

Be good to yourself throughout the transition process.

"Paddle with the current."

– Kris Kristofferson

"Move with the flow."

– Oprah Winfrey

Expect some highs and some lows in retirement, but try not to get discouraged. Think of your first year of retirement as a trial-and-error period. Retirement is a time to explore and experiment. Try something once. If you don't like it then simply move on. There are no failures, just learning.

"Retirement is a work in progress."

– Pete Sampras

"'Don't be afraid. Change is such a beautiful thing', said the Butterfly."
– Sabrina Newly

The Road of Life

"Take the road less traveled."

– Robert Frost

"Take the road most traveled—maybe they know something you don't."
– Tom Weber

"If you come to a fork in the road, take it."

– Yogi Berra

"I took the road less traveled. Now, I don't know where the hell I am!"

– Ziggy

"It's your road and yours alone. Others may walk it with you, but no one can walk it for you."

– Anonymous

"Leave the road, take the trails!"

– Pythagore

"Even if you're on the right track, you'll get run over if you just sit there."
– Will Rogers

"Do not go where the path may lead, go instead where there is no path and leave a trail."

– Ralph Waldo Emerson

"Retirement is not the end of the road. It is the beginning of the open highway."

– Anonymous

"Of all the paths you take in life, make sure that some of them are dirt."
– John Muir

"Normality is a paved road. It's comfortable to walk, but no flowers grow on it."
– Vincent Van Gogh

"The road not taken was not taken for a reason. Trust that you are right where you need to be."
– Tumblr

"How many roads must a man walk down before he admits he's lost?"
– Anonymous

"Never follow anyone else's path, unless you're in the woods and you're lost."
– Ellen DeGeneres

"Sometimes the road less traveled is less traveled for a reason."
– Jerry Seinfeld

Senior Moments

Where did I put my car keys? Moments of forgetfulness or absentmindedness in later life are euphemistically called Senior Moments. As we continue to age we tend to experience these momentary memory lapses more often. Embrace your Senior Moments. Laugh them off. They're not a sign of mental decay. They are a normal part of aging. However, like any problem, if it causes you concern it might be time to see your doctor.

"Senility ain't so bad. I can wrap my own birthday presents."
– Refrigerator Magnet

"When you lost your car keys in high school—why don't you call it a 'Junior Moment?'"
– Ashton Applewhite

"I forgot where I put my keys…and why I needed them."
– The Lockhorns by Bunny Hoest and John Reiner

"Do brain farts smell?"
– Bumper Sticker

"I have a photographic memory. Unfortunately, it no longer offers same day service."
– Anonymous

"There are three signs of old age. Loss of memory I forget the other two."
– Red Skelton

"First you forget names, then you forget faces; then you forget to zip your fly, then you forget to unzip your fly."
– Branch Rickey

"Grandma says she's seen it all, done it all, and heard it all. She just can't remember it all."

– Bill Keane

"You know, I have found a new way to get high and stay spaced out for hours on end, and the government can't stop me… it's called senility."

– Robert Anton Wilson

"Nothing is more responsible for the good old days than a bad memory."

– Robert Benchley

"You're not senile. You're Retiremental!"

– Tom Weber

Self-Care

"Self-discipline is self-caring."

– M. Scott Peck

"The most powerful relationship you will ever have is the relationship with yourself."

– Steve Maraboli

"To thine own self be true."

– William Shakespeare

"If your passion doesn't include yourself, it is incomplete."

– Jack Kornfield

"Each of us makes his on weather, determines the color of the skies in the emotional universe which he inhabits."

– Fulton Sheen

"If you don't take care of yourself, the undertaker will overtake that responsibility for you."

– Carrie Latet

"Today it's up to you to create the peacefulness you long for."

– Fortune Cookie

"We need to do a better job of putting ourselves higher on our own 'To-do' List."

– Michelle Obama

"Lighten up on yourself. No one is perfect. Gently accept your humanness."

– Deborah Day

"Self-care is never selfish, but it may feel that way when you live a frenzied life."

– Arthur P. Ciaramicoli

"Of all the judgments we pass in life, none is more important than the judgment we pass on ourselves."

– Nathaniel Branden

"An empty lantern provides no light. Self-care is the fuel that allows your light to shine brightly."

– Anonymous

"Taking care of yourself doesn't mean me first, it means me too."
– L.R. Knost

Your Ship Has Come In!

"I am the captain of my ship and the master of my fate."

– Anonymous

"A ship in harbor is safe, but that is not what ships are built for."

– John A. Shedd

"Sail away from the safe harbor. Catch the trade winds in your sails. Explore. Dream. Discover."

– Mark Twain

"I can't change the direction of the wind, but I can adjust my sails to always reach my destination."

– Jimmy Dean

"Whatever floats your boat."

– Button

"If a man knows not to which port he sails, no wind is favorable."

– Seneca

"Neither should a ship rely on one small anchor, nor should life rest on a single hope."

– Epictetus

"I am not afraid of storms, for I am learning how to sail my ship."
– Louisa May Alcott

"A man without goals is like a ship without a rudder."
– Thomas Carlyle

"I love to sail forbidden seas, and land on barbarous coasts."
– Herman Melville

"Find a beautiful place and drop anchor."
– Anonymous

"Life is a shipwreck, but we must not forget to sing in the life boats."
– Voltaire

"If your ship doesn't come in, swim out to meet it!"
– Jonathan Winters

Simplify

"Be a curator of your life. Slowly cut things out until you're left only with what you love, with what's necessary, with what makes you happy."
– Leo Babauta

"Our life is frittered away by detail. Simplify. Simplify. Simplify."
– Henry David Thoreau

"There must be more to life than having everything."
– Maurice Sendak

"In the process of letting go, you will lose many things from the past, but you will find yourself."
– Deepak Chopra

"Have nothing in your house that you do not know to be useful or believe to be beautiful."
– William Morris

"Re-create the carefree conditions of youth by jettisoning the things that aren't necessary to your basic well-being."
– Rolf Potts

"Treasure your relationships, not your possessions."
– Anthony J. D'Angelo

"The bare necessities, the simple bare necessities, forget about your worries and your strife."
– Terry Gilkyson

"Materialistic people are seldom the happiest people because they want too much."

– Dan Buettner

"All you need is less."

– Anonymous

"Train yourself to let go of everything you fear to lose."

– Yoda

"One does not accumulate, but eliminate. It is not daily increase, but daily decrease. The height of cultivation always runs to simplicity."

– Bruce Lee

"It is vain to do with more what can be done with less."

– William of Ockham

Death Cleaning is a Swedish term for making your home clutter free and orderly in the later stages of life in order to decrease the burden and stress on your loved ones.

Kon-Mari is the art of ruthlessly decluttering your life by purging everything, except for your most essential possessions that spark joy.

Wabi-Sabi is the acceptance and appreciation of the imperfect and impermanent nature of all things.

"The best things in life aren't things."
– Art Buchwald

Contradiction Alert!
"Tossing out things you don't really need is trendy, but are we losing a part of ourselves in the process? Some possessions are irreplaceable treasures."

– Anonymous

Sitting

"Sit down whenever you can."

— Leslie Nielsen

"I still believe that sitting down and reading a book is the best way to really learn something."

— Eric Schmidt

"Sitting is the gateway of truth to total liberation."

— Dogen

"Sometimes it feels so good to just sit by yourself, relax, and not talk to anyone."

— Kristen Butler

"My get up and go has changed to sit down and stop."

— By Fred Sahner

"If you feel like doing some work, sit down and wait until that feeling goes away."

— Calvin (Bill Watterson)

"Life's a bench."

— Bumper Sticker

"I like work it fascinates me. I can sit and look at it for hours."

— Jerome K. Jerome

"I do most of my work sitting down; that's where I shine."

— Robert Benchley

"Never be afraid to sit awhile and think."

– Lorraine Hansberry

"My favorite yoga position is sitting on the sofa with a glass of wine."
– Refrigerator Magnet

Contradiction Alert!
"Footprints on the sands of time are not made by sitting down."
– Proverb

"The goal of retirement is to live off your assets—not on them."
– Frank Eberhart

Sleep

"As a child going to bed early was a punishment, as a retiree it's a reward!"
– Anonymous

"Don't give up on your dreams. Keep sleeping."
– Tumblr

"Find your 'Slumber Number'. There is no magic number for hours of sleep per night, but a general guideline is 8."
– Mayo Clinic

"Generally, the amount of sleep you need decreases as you get older."
– Dr. Andrew Weil

Avoid becoming nocturnal.

"What if sleep is an addiction and tiredness is just a withdrawal symptom?"
– Meme

"Every woman's dream is that a man will take her in his arms, throw her into bed…and clean the house while she sleeps."
– Iain Morland

"Get sleep. Eat clean. Drink water. Exercise. Repeat."
– Anonymous

"Go to sleep in peace. God is awake."

– Victor Hugo

"Without sleep we become tall two year olds."

– Button

Create a Worry Journal. After dinner, write in your journal about bothersome issues and what you could do to resolve them. Then close the book on your worries until the following day.

"Never under any circumstances take a sleeping pill and a laxative on the same night."
– Dave Barry

Contradiction Alert!
"Not all closed eyes are sleeping nor open eyes are seeing."
– Fortune Cookie

Slow Down

"Slow down, you move too fast.
You got to make the morning last.
Just kicking down the cobble stones.
Looking for fun and feelin' groovy."

– Simon and Garfunkel

"Remember the Tortoise beat the Hare."

– Tom Weber

"Squeeze the tube slowly, because once the toothpaste is out, it's hard to get back in."

– Anonymous

"Stop and smell the roses—and the rose'."

– Tom Weber

"I'm in a hurry and don't know why
Run and run until life's no fun
All we really gotta do is live and die
And I'm in a hurry and don't know why."

– Alabama

"The faster we travel, the less there is to see."

– Helen Hayes

"Life moves pretty fast. If you don't stop and look around once in a while, you could miss it."

– Ferris Bueller

"Spend 30 minutes taking a 5 minute walk."

– Anonymous

"No hurry! No worry!"

– Tom Weber's Retirement Motto

"In today's rush, we all think too much—seek too much—want too much and forget about the joy of just being."

– Eckhart Tolle

"Not Fast. Not Furious."

– Tee Shirt

"I don't want to hurry it. That itself is a poisonous twentieth-century attitude. When you want to hurry something, that means you no longer care about it and want to get on to other things."

– Robert M. Pirg

"It does not matter how slowly you go so long as you do not stop."
– Confucius

Contradiction Alert!
"I never said all that shit."
– Confucius (Bumper Sticker)

Smile

"Smile. It's free therapy."

– Douglas Horton

"You gotta be able to smile through the bullshit."

– Tupac

"Create a 'Smile File'. Fill it with your favorite comics, photos, and quotes that are guaranteed to make you smile."

– Tom Weber

"Smile though your heart is aching
Smile even though it's breaking
When there are clouds in the sky, you'll get by
If you smile through your fear and sorrow
Smile and maybe tomorrow
You'll see the sun come shining through for you."

– Charles Chaplin

"A smile is your passport into the hearts of others."

– Fortune Cookie

"You're never fully dressed without a smile."
– Charles Strouse

"Don't cry because it's over, smile because it happened."
– Dr. Seuss

"And when the evening comes, we smile
So much of life ahead
We'll find a place where there's room to grow
And yes, we've just begun."
– Roger S. Nichols and Paul H. Williams

"Your smile is your logo."
– Tom Weber

Contradiction Alert!
"Start every day with a smile and get it over with."
– W.C. Fields

"Never trust people who smile constantly.
They're either selling something or not very bright."
– Laurel K. Hamilton

Solitude

"Practice solitude 10 minutes a day, and if you're busy—practice solitude 20 minutes a day."

– Anonymous

"Solitude is where I place my chaos to rest and awaken my inner peace."

– Nikki Rowe

"You cannot be lonely if you like the person you're alone with."

– Wayne W Dyer

"The cure for loneliness is solitude."

– Anne Morrow Lindberg

"I live in that solitude which is painful in youth, but delicious in the years of maturity."

– Albert Einstein

"Even Superman had his 'Fortress of Solitude'."

– Tom Weber

Spiritual Awakening

"What do you hold sacred?"

– Anonymous

"God has a plan for your retirement."

– Billy Graham

"Life is full of miracles, but they're not always the ones we pray for."

– Eve Arden

"God's retirement plan is out of this world."

– Anonymous

"Where should we live after retirement?"

– Anonymous

**"Use the experience of aging as a stimulus
for spiritual awakening and growth."**
– Dr. Andrew Weil

Spontaneity

"Plan to be spontaneous tomorrow."

– Steven Wright

"Spontaneity is the spice of life, not drama."

– Anonymous

"No matter how many plans you make or how much in control you are, life is always winging it."

– Carroll Bryant

"Warning: May spontaneously break into song."

– Bumper Sticker

"How do people my age plan spontaneous trips to Thailand. I can barely afford a spontaneous soft pretzel."

– Meme

"Be spontaneous, but think about it first."

– Bumper Sticker

"Be spontaneous, be creative, go out and have fun, let things happen naturally."

– Conor McGregor

"Over planning kills magic."
– Bumper Sticker

Contradiction Alert!
"Being spontaneous at times is a must."
– Ryan Hansen

"Whenever, I start feeling spontaneous, my bank account quietly reminds me to calm down."
– Tumblr

Stillness

You do not have to be doing something all the time.

"Teach us to care and not to care. Teach us to sit still."
– T. S. Eliot

"Within you, there is a stillness and sanctuary to which you can retreat at any time and be yourself."
– Hermann Hesse

Stillness brings a sense of calm to your daily life. Reduce angst. Sleep better. Increase energy.

"You don't have to be doing something to be doing something."
– Tom Weber

"In the midst of movement and chaos, keep stillness inside of you."
– Deepak Chopra

Contradiction Alert!
"Many a false step was made by standing still."
–Anonymous

Swear Words in Retirement

- Meeting - Commute
- Appointment - Work
- Job - Boss
- Career - Alarm Clock
- Budget - Office

Technology

Be tech savvy. Keep up with new technology.

Have an active social life online and off.

Use technology and social media to stay connected with distant friends and relatives, but remember that actual face to face time is the best FaceTime.

"A computer once beat me at chess, but it was no match for me at kick boxing."
— Emo Philips

"Dance like no one is watching, because they're not, they're checking their phones."
— Anonymous

"When I was your age, television was called books."
— William Goldman

"Old robots are becoming more human and young humans are becoming more like robots."
— Lorin Morgan-Richards

"Live with technology, not through technology."

– Abhijit Naskar

Watch out for the TV trap. Reconsider your relationship with your television.

"Try a 'No News Diet'. Limit your intake of bad news by turning the channel."

– Tom Weber

"You control your technology; it doesn't control you."
– Fr. Nels Gjengdahl

Time

"All we have to decide is what to do with the time that is given to us."

– Gandalf

"Tempus Fugit! (Time flies) Especially during retirement!"

– Tom Weber

"The bad news is time flies. The good news is you're the pilot."

– Michael Althsuler

"You don't find time for the things you enjoy—you make time."

– Herb

"Flow" through time. Flow is being so engaged and emerged with the object of your involvement that you find yourself totally loosing yourself in the moment.

"Time is the truest form of wealth. And the beauty is, we are all born equally rich in time."

– Rolf Potts

"Time you enjoy wasting is not wasted time."

– Anonymous

"Life is like a roll of toilet paper, it goes faster when you near the end."

– Bumper Sticker

"You rarely have time for everything you want in this life, so you need to make choices. And hopefully your choices can come from a deep sense of who you are."

– Mr. Rogers

"Ch-ch-ch-ch-changes
Turn and face the strange
Ch-ch-changes
Pretty soon now you're gonna get older
Time may change me
But I can't trace time."

– David Bowie

"There will come a time when you believe everything is finished—that will be the beginning."

– Louis L'Amour

"Time cools all jets."

– Wall Hanging

"The trouble is, you think you have time."

– Buddha

"There's a difference between time filling and fulfilling activities."
– Anonymous

Time Travel

"What do we want? Time travel! When do we want it? Irrelevant."

– Meme

"When you are dissatisfied and would like to go back to youth, think of Algebra."

– Will Rogers

"Photography is a form of time travel."

– Anonymous

"Time travel? Love to try it, but never seem to find the time."

– Anonymous

"Some days I wish I could go back in life. Not to change anything, but to feel a few things twice."

– Anonymous

"I put instant coffee in a microwave oven and almost went back in time."
— Steven Wright

"If time is money, an ATM is a time machine."
— Meme

"I would willingly stand at street corners, hat in hand, begging every passersby to drop their unused minutes into it."
— Bernard Berenson

"I don't always time travel to the past, but when I do, I did."
— Meme

"When I'm old, how much would I be willing to pay to travel back in time and relive the moment that I'm experiencing right now?"
— Muneeb Ali

"Create your own Time Machine with a bottle of wine and a high school yearbook."
— Tom Weber

Today

"Today is a good day for a good day."

– Refrigerator Magnet

"You better live each day like it's your last cause one day you're gonna be right."

– Ray Charles

"Nothing is more important than this day."

– Goethe

"Dear Universe, I am totally open to some awesome today!"

– Anonymous

"Sometimes you will never know the value of a moment until it becomes a memory."

– Dr. Seuss

"Today, while the blossoms still cling to the vine
I'll taste your strawberries, I'll drink your sweet wine
A million tomorrows shall all pass away.
'Ere I forget all the joy that is mine, today."

– John Denver

"Don't judge each day by the harvest you reap, but by the seeds you plant."
– Robert Louis Stevenson

"It's a beautiful day. Don't let it get away."
– U2

"The only way to live is by accepting each minute as an unrepeatable miracle."
– Tara Brach

"Make each day your masterpiece."
– John Wooden

"Now's the day, and now's the hour."
– Robert Burns

"Each new day is trembling with potential."
– Woody Harrelson

"Look around. Look around. How lucky we are to be alive right now."
– Lin Manuel Miranda

"Who we are in the present includes who we were in the past."
– Mr. Rogers.

"I want today to be so awesome that yesterday will be jealous."
– Rick Bartkowitz

Tomorrow

"Tomorrow will come. Go ahead and buy green tomatoes."

– Anonymous

"People don't realize that the future is just now, but later."

– Russell Brand

"The future will be better tomorrow."

– Dan Quayle

"The way to give God a good laugh is to tell him your plans for the future."

– Woody Allen

"Today is yesterday's tomorrow."

– Tom Weber

"Que sera, sera
Whatever will be, will be
The future's not ours to see
Que sera, sera
What will be, will be."

– Jay Livingston and Ray Evans

"The future belongs to those who believe in the beauty of their dreams."

– Eleanor Roosevelt

"When the past becomes the present you lose the future."

– Anonymous

"Nothing is inevitable."

– Button

"Tomorrow is often the busiest day of the week."

– Spanish Proverb

"When you have one foot in the future and the other in the past, you piss on the present."

– Dan Harris

"It is a mistake to look too far ahead. The chain of destiny can only be grasped one link at a time."

– Winston Churchill

"Seize the day. Put no trust is tomorrow."

– Horace

"The best prophet of the future is the past."

– Fortune Cookie

"Your future depends on many things, but mostly on you."

– Frank Tyger

"Life always offers you a second chance. It's called tomorrow."
– Poster

Travel

"Not all those who wander are lost."

– J. R. R. Tolkien

"I'm not lost. I'm exploring."

– Bumper Sticker

"Thanks to the interstate highway system, it is now possible to travel from coast to coast without seeing anything."

– Charles Kuralt

"A man on foot, on horseback, or on a bicycle will see more, feel more, enjoy more in one mile than the motorized tourists can in a hundred miles."

– Edward Abbey

"Always—always—always take the scenic route."

– Tom Weber

"Better to see something once, than hear about it a thousand times."

– Anonymous

"Travel leaves you speechless—then turns you into a storyteller."

– Ibu Battuta

"There was nowhere to go but everywhere."

– Jack Kerouac

"Me: 'I want to travel'. Bank Account: 'Like…to the backyard?'"

– Iain Morland

"For my part, I travel not to go anywhere, but to go. I travel for travel's sake."

– Anonymous

"Become a temporary local."

– Rick Steves

"Un-plan a chunk of your planned trip. Leave room for spontaneity, serendipity, and uncertainty."

– Tom Weber

"Once a year, go somewhere you've never been before."

– Dalai Lama

There are literally thousands of travel discounts. Planes. Trains. Buses. Cars. Cruises. Hotels. Restaurants. Theaters. Museums. Aquariums. Zoos. Parks. Most businesses don't advertise them—so don't be afraid to ask.

"My favorite thing is to go where I've never been."

– Diane Arbus

"It's better to travel and get lost, than never to travel at all."
– Anonymous

Unplug

"Sometimes, the best way to recharge is to unplug."

– Chris Butler

"Disconnecting from our technology to reconnect with ourselves is absolutely essential for wisdom."

– Arianna Huffington

"Burn your computer. Blow up your TY. Bludgeon your cell phone. Breathe deeply. This, my friends, is the secret to inner-peace."

– Brian Vaszily

"Take a technology sabbath. Detox from all social media."

– Anonymous

"So please, oh please, we beg, we pray, go throw your TV set away, and in its place you can install a lovely bookshelf on the wall."

– Roald Dahl

"Disengage electronically after 3 p.m."

– Dr. Andrew Weil

"Being connected to everything has disconnected us from ourselves and the preciousness of this present moment."

– L. M. Browning

"Keep calm and take a break from Social Media."

– Poster

"Your inbox can wait—your life can't."

– Tom Weber

"Life is what happens between Wi-Fi signals."

– Anonymous

"Those who continually lose themselves in electronic distractions, will eventually find themselves with realistic frustrations."

– Tom Weber

"Almost everything will work again if you unplug it for a few minutes, including you."
– Anne Lamott

Contradiction Alert!
"Anybody have plans to stare at their phones somewhere exciting this weekend?"
– Anonymous

Un-Retirement:

From Retiree to Employee – a.k.a. Boomer-Boomerang

"If you experience 'Retiree's Remorse'—retire from retirement."
– Tom Weber

Work Related Reasons Why to Un-Retire…

-You miss the sense of fulfillment.

-You miss the challenges.

-You miss the social interactions. You miss the paychecks.

Retirement Related Reasons Why to Un-Retire…

-You're bored being retired.

-Your spouse or partner still works.

-You're dissatisfied with your life of leisure.

"If your previous career keeps calling you back – answer the call or change your phone number."
– Tom Weber

Vacation

"It's bad manners to keep a vacation waiting!"

– Anonymous

"The only cure for 'Vacation-itis' is a vacation."

– Tom Weber

"How about a 'Gray-cation!' Take a trip with a group of other retirees."

– Tom Weber

"What about a 'Day-cation!' A one-day trip to a new local spot."

– Tom Weber

"Hey, Foodies, how about 'Gourmet-cation!' A trip that focuses on dining!"

– Tom Weber

"Try taking a 'Stay-cation!' Do something vacation-like at home."

– Anonymous

"Laughter is an instant vacation."
– Milton Berle

Contradiction Alert!
"Create a life you don't need to vacation from."
– Rob Hill

Volunteer

"Not all super heroes wear capes."

– Alex M.O.R.P.H.

"Being willing is not enough; we must do."

– Leonardo da Vinci

Sometimes a voluntary position chooses you. Listen for your calling. Find a need and fill it. Volunteering enhances life satisfaction and personal well-being. You will get more than you give.

"Volunteering is a vaccine against stagnation and boredom."

– Anonymous

"Some people dream big, others wish to do something simpler, but all action devoted to helping others matters."

– Robin Ryan

Look before you leap into a volunteer position. Make sure it's a good fit before you commit your time and talents. Volunteer with your spouse or partner. Co-volunteers are a good source for potential friends. You are going to get a lot of offers and requests. Be discerning. Do not over volunteer. Try informal volunteering like helping a neighbor or a friend with a chore.

"The best way to find yourself is to lose yourself in the service of others."
– Gandhi

"The noblest question in the world is, 'What good may I do in it?'"
– Poor Richard

Any charitable, philanthropic, religious, or non-profit organization would be glad to have you!

"It's easy to make a buck. It's a lot tougher to make a difference."
– Tom Brokaw

The online sites www.volunteermatch.org, www.idealist.org, and www.nationalservice.gov/ programs/ senior-corps are great sources for volunteer activities in your area.

Wellness

"Health is a state of body. Wellness is a state of being."

– J. Stanford

"Wellness is the complete integration of body, mind, and spirit—the realization that everything we do, think, feel, and believe has an effect on our state of well-being."

– Greg Anderson

"If you think wellness is expensive—then try illness."

– Meme

"Well-being comes through action, not through prayer."

– Dalai Lama

"When 'I' is replaced by 'We' even 'illness' becomes 'wellness'."

– Malcolm X

"Grow through what you go through."

– Greeting Card

"To be healthy as a whole—wellness has a role."

– Bumper Sticker

"I pity the fool who doesn't get a regular massage."
– Mr. T

Wisdom

"Knowledge is not wisdom until it is shared."

– Gary West

"In our youth, we learn. With our age, we understand."

– Button

"The whiter the hair becomes the more ready people are to believe what you say."

– Bertrand Russell

"You do the Hokey-Pokey, and you turn yourself around, that's what it's all about."

– Charles Mack

"You don't have to be in 'Who's Who' to know what's what."

– Sam Levenson

"Whenever I'm about to do something, I think, 'Would an idiot do that?' And if they would, I do not do that thing."

– Dwight Schrute: from "The Office"

"A little gray hair is a small price to pay for all this accumulated wisdom."

– Anonymous

Contradiction Alert!

"The older I grow the more I distrust
the familiar doctrine that age brings wisdom."
– H. L. Mencken

Worry

"Worry is the misuse of the imagination."

– Dan Zadra

"Worry often gives a small thing a big shadow."

– Swedish Proverb

"Worry never robs tomorrow of its sorrow, it only saps today of its joy."

– Leo F. Buscaglia

"In every life, we have some trouble,
but when you worry you make it double.
Don't worry, be happy."

– Bobby McFerrin

"Don't worry about the world coming to an end today. It is already tomorrow in Australia."

– Charles Schultz

"Well, at least you don't have to worry about dying young."
– Tom Weber

Exercise

"Blah. Blah. Blah. Go workout."

— Button

"Exercise is a retirement requirement."

— Tom Weber

Think of exercise as a form of medicine.

"Running late is my cardio."

— Refrigerator Magnet

"There is no exercise better for the heart than reaching down and lifting people up."

— John Andrew Holmes

"First we inspire them, then we perspire them."

— Jack Leanne

"Want to get fit? Sell your couch."

— Ericka Bolstad

"Take time every day to grab some endorphins."

— Gary Owens

Never too late to get fit. Do what your body permits. Fitness doesn't happen overnight.

"Exercise is a poor man's cosmetic surgery."

— Anonymous

"Yoga is my favorite way to pretend to work out."
– Button

Contradiction Alert!
"Whenever the urge to exercise comes upon me,
I lie down for a while and it passes."
– Robert Maynard Hutchins

"Abs are great, but have you tried donuts?"
– Button

"I'm so unfamiliar with the gym, I call it James!"
– Ellen DeGeneres

"To get back my youth I would do anything in the world—except take exercise!"
– Oscar Wilde

"Exercise? I thought you said extra fries!"
– Anonymous

Yesterday

"You must have the courage to let go of the past if you are going to grasp the future."

— Anonymous

"Used-to-be's don't count anymore."

— Neil Diamond

"Don't let yesterday use up too much of today."

— Cherokee Proverb

"My yesterdays walk with me."

— William Golding

"If you hold on to the old things, you will not experience the new."

— Joseph Campbell

"Whenever I think of the past, it brings back so many memories."
— Steven Wright

Young

"Never forget what it was to be young."

— Anonymous

"You're only young once, but you can be immature indefinitely."

— Ogden Nash

"May your hands always be busy
May your feet always be swift
May you have a strong foundation
When the winds of changes shift
May your heart always be joyful
And may your song always be sung
May you stay forever young."

– Bob Dylan

"I want to die young at an advanced age."

– Max Lerner

"I believe we can keep ourselves young by surrounding ourselves with things that make us feel young."

– David De Notaris

"Today is the youngest you will ever be."

– Anonymous

"Ever notice that you have to get old before people start saying how young you look."

– Joey Adams

"Youth has no age."

– Pablo Picasso

"This is a youth-oriented society, and the joke is on them because youth is a disease from which we all recover."

– Dorothy Fuldheim

"Except for the occasional heart attack, I feel as young as I ever did."
– Robert Benchley

Zest

"The robust shall inherit the earth. Be old and be bold!"

– Tom Weber

"Whether we live to a vigorous old age lies not so much in our stars or our genes as in ourselves."

– George Vaillant

"Don't act your age. Act like the inner young person you have always been."

– J A. West

"Put a dash of zest into everything you do."

– Tom Weber

"Zip-a-dee-doo-dah, zip-a-dee-ay
My, oh, my, what a wonderful day
Plenty of sunshine headin' my way
Zip-a-dee-doo-dah, zip-a-dee-ay!"

– James Baskett

"Zeal is a volcano, on the peak of which the grass of indecisiveness does not grow."

– Khalil Gibran

"What hunger is in relation to food——zest is in relation to life."
– Bertrand Russell

"Without zest, what is life? Just waiting for death?"
– Rajneesh

Random Retirement-Isms

"I called the incontinence hotline. They asked if I could hold."
– Anonymous

"Time is the final currency. How do you plan to spend it?"
– David Crosby

"The time to relax is when you don't have time for it."
– Sydney J. Harris

"So when is this old enough to know better supposed to kick in."
– Anonymous

"When I grow up, I want to be a little boy."
– Joseph Heller

"Invent your world. Surround yourself with people, color, sounds, and work that nourish you."
– Sark

"Edit your life frequently and ruthlessly. It's your masterpiece after all."
– Nathan W. Morris

"I may be an antique like the (Rolling) Stones, but antiques are valuable."
– Billy Joel

"Old age is the only disease you don't looked forward to being cured of."
– From *Citizen Kane*

"The aging process has you firmly in its grasp if you never get the urge to throw a snowball."
– Doug Larson

"The secret of staying young is to live honestly, eat slowly, and lie about your age."

– Lucille Ball

"Begin at once to live, and count each separate day as a separate life."

– Seneca

"And now, the end is near…
And so I face the final curtain
My friends, I'll say it clear…
I'll state my case of which I'm certain
I've lived a life that's full…
I traveled each and every highway
But more, much more than this
I did it my way."

– Paul Anka

"I'm maturing. That's better than aging. You enjoy different things."

– Ted Turner

"The young talk about sex. The middle-aged talk about business. The old talk about their operations."

– Pablo Jury

"It's inappropriate to always be age inappropriate."
– Tom Weber

Random Retiremental-Isms

"Don't mess with old people. We don't get to this age by being stupid."
— Words on a Sweat Shirt

"The greatest wealth is health."
— Virgil

"A self that goes on changing is a self that goes on living."
— Virginia Woolf

"Heck with the fountain of youth I'm looking for the fountain of health,"
— Tom Weber

"Don't just lean in. Go all in."
— Tom Weber

"Perennials' are ever-blooming, relevant people of all ages who live in the present time, know what's happening in the world, stay current with technology, and have friends of all ages."
— Gina Pell

"We are always the same age on the inside."
— Gertrude Stein

Relaxation skills can be developed. Edmund Jacobson, a pioneer in the research of the connection between physical tension and mental wellbeing, developed the progressive muscle relaxation technique. Find a quiet space. Set aside 10 – 15 minutes. Lie down. Take deep slow breaths. Clinch, hold, and release every muscle in your body. Start with your toes, up to your head, and out to your fingertips. Before you know it your entire body will be relaxed and tension free.

"Declare a 'Pajama Day!' Stay in your Pjs all day long."
— Brenda Hillard

"You know you're getting old when all the names in your black book have M.D. after them."
— Arnold Palmer

"Nothing is impossible, the word itself says, 'I'm possible.'"
— Audrey Hepburn

"Dream as if you'll live forever. Live as if you'll die today."
— James Dean

"I got into the bathtub this morning without taking my clothes off… which is OK, because I forgot to turn the water on."
— Anonymous

"The best thing one can do when it's raining is to let it rain."
— Henry Wadsworth Longfellow

"Be strong enough to stand alone, smart enough to know when you need help, and brave enough to ask for it."
— Ziad K. Abdelnour

"What if, what if ran away with why not?"
— Anonymous

"Non I want to know is where Ihe gonna die so Ioen never go there.
— Charlie Munger

"Relax like a cat. Play like a dog."
— Anonymous

"May all your 'Wish I had's.' turn into 'Glad I did's!'"
— Tom Weber

Epilogue

My final piece of advice is this: if your retirement doesn't seem to be going as planned or as smoothly as you would like—seek assistance. Call a trusted friend. Text a family member.

Your support system is there for just such a situation. They will willingly and gratefully help you—just as you would assist them if the roles were reversed. Let your friends be your friends. Let your family be your family.

Self-reliance is a positive quality, but not when it hinders you from seeking needed assistance. Don't let your self-reliance aand your rugged individualism hold you back. Asking for assistance is not a weakness of character and will fix your problem—thus enabling you to retake control of your situation, your retirement, and your life.